MICHAEL G. THOMAS JR.

BL♥CK FINANCIAL CULTURE

BUILDING WEALTH FROM THE INSIDE OUT

ISBN: 979-8-9878908-0-6

This book is designed solely to provide education
on money mindset, wealth building, wholeness,
empathy, and compassion. It is recommended
that readers seek explicit guidance from a financial
coach, counselor, therapist, or planner regarding
their financial situation. The reader bears full
responsibility for any outcomes resulting from
actions taken based on the information presented
in this book. All quotes included in this book are
taken from public domain sources.

DEDICATION

I would like to dedicate this book to Tiara Tenee Thomas.
You were and still are my reservoir of unlimited hope,
unbridled inspiration, and unfailing love.

Love, even when it's inconvenient.

Mother to Son
By Langston Hughes

Well, son, I'll tell you:
Life for me ain't been no crystal stair.
It's had tacks in it,
And splinters,
And boards torn up,
And places with no carpet on the floor—
Bare;
But all the time
I'se been a'climbin' on,
And reachin' landin's,
And turnin' corners,
And sometimes goin' in the dark,
Where there ain't been no light.
So boy, don't you turn back;
Don't you sit down on the steps,
'Cause you finds it's kinder hard;
Don't you fall now—
For I'se still goin', honey,
I'se still climbin',
And life for me ain't been no crystal stair.

A NOTE FROM MICHAEL'S MOTHER

I always knew Michael would amount to something, but earning a doctoral degree in financial planning from the University of Georgia never struck my mind. Ironically enough, he had profound struggles with math as a child. When Michael was in first grade, there were times we'd stay up until 2 in the morning doing math homework. As the young folks like to say, the struggle was real.

He might get mad at you if I tell this story, but I will anyway. This one time, we were trying to teach Michael how to count. He couldn't remember the number three to save his life. Well, there was one afternoon when we were working on his numbers. He had to have been four at the time. I had him count and he'd say "one, two," and then go completely blank. After about the third try, his younger sister, who was three, would say "three" whenever he'd get stuck. He got so mad and tried to make his sister leave the room. Then we'd start over and the same thing would happen. We laugh about it now. But it was a sign of things to come.

Because of those early struggles, we never looked forward to parent-teacher conferences. It was the same routine. We'd walk in, engage in some light-hearted conversation, and dive right into their concerns. "We are not sure if Michael can do the work at the next grade level," we were told. This went on for several years before things really started to click for him. How? We don't know, but we are glad that it did. The fact that he's an educator, entrepreneur, financial coach, speaker and now author just blows my mind.

I can tell you that Michael grew up modestly. While we spent the majority of our lives in Gary, IN, there were military-based stops in Hawaii and North Carolina, as his father served in the United States Marine Corps. When Michael's dad and I divorced, we moved to the Aetna community in Gary, IN, where I raised Michael and his sister the best way I could.

Michael was quiet growing up – very respectful and no trouble at all. Honestly, I couldn't have asked for a better son. I instilled a lot of values in him that he retained – forgiveness, compassion, and a can-do attitude. I had a singular request of him, which he greatly exceeded – be a great person and give your all in whatever you do.

Sometimes, I feel like Michael is the parent, and I have to remind him and I who the captain is. "Hold on now! I brought you into this world. I'll take you out!"

In all seriousness, Michael has been a godsend, and as it relates to this book, I have learned so much about finances from him. He might tell you that he learned from my experiences. He watched as I struggled to make ends meet, and while I was disciplined with my work ethic, I wasn't as strong-willed when it came to my earnings. *You only live once,* I told myself, long before Drake made it a *motto.* I also had an unhealthy vice – the casino, or "The Boats," as we called them in Gary.

If I'm being totally vulnerable, the divorce challenged my kids and I. Where I dealt with coping mechanisms, Michael dealt with culture shock. I vividly remember when he asked me, "Mom, why am I in school with all of these *brown* people?", which spoke to his military upbringing. Gary, located in North-West Indiana, also brought conversations about gang activity. Before Michael went to school, I asked him, "Which gang are you a part of?"

"The Thomas gang," he would tell me.

Sometimes, I wish I could have afforded a U-Haul to pack up our belongings and move back to North Carolina. Still, we persevered, largely because all of our support networks were in the Hoosier State. Despite all of Gary's flaws, we needed to be close to family and friends to navigate the road ahead.

Highways are often used as an allegory for financial success, and my son has been a driving force in that regard. I've learned how to save money for a rainy day without the fear and worry that comes with unexpected financial shocks. I've learned how to improve my credit score, refinance high interest loans, and pay off debt. Michael's advice and bottomless patience has yielded a new home, a savings account with actual money in it, an excellent credit score, and a positive wealth position.

The beautiful thing about my son is that he has never browbeaten me or forced his perspectives and intellect on finances on me – even when I made financial mistakes. He leads by example. He's been driving his Toyota Camry for 18 years, which his wife affectionately calls Panda because it's white with black spots due to chipped paint. And he won't get a paint job. He jokes that a paint job costs more than his car is worth. Now, I love cars. But watching Michael drive around for nearly two decades without a car note makes me think twice about getting another car whenever I get that new car itch.

Maybe that's the motto of the Thomas gang – "surviving to thriving." Our family went from struggles in school and society to gracefully growing and navigating through life. Michael isn't much of a talker, which makes his words more profound when he shares them with the world. They don't just touch your mind; they touch your heart. And if he can change this stubborn old lady's heart at this stage of life, I know he can change yours.

Happy reading,

Lisa Smith-Rodriguez

CONTENTS

1.

LET'S BE CLEAR ABOUT ONE THING...

Money without wisdom is a liability.

My reasons for writing this book are less about money and more about you. Money is not the main thing. YOU are.

Say it with me. *I am the main thing.* Say it again. I am the MAIN thing.

Maybe... You don't believe it yet. Do you? Alright. Put the book down. Close your eyes. With each deep breath you take, say it again, and again. Allow the seed of you being invaluable beyond measure to exist within you.

That idea is the framework of this entire book. It's important to believe in yourself and your own worth, and to treat yourself with kindness and compassion. By doing so, you can build an unshakable positive self-image and increase your overall sense of well-being. A healthy relationship with self leads to a better relationship with money.

Let's be honest. Without a solid sense of self worth, it becomes incredibly convenient to seek external validation. Instead of turning inward, we resort to seeking tangible things to represent love of self, our families and communities. Think about it. How many of us as parents have worked tirelessly to give our children the things we didn't have, only to realize that all our kids needed was more of our time, warmth and affection?

Despite spending precious time and money on material possessions to satisfy ourselves, we often end up feeling empty inside. Rather than examining this feeling of emptiness, many of us resort to doubling down, similar to gamblers in a casino, hoping to achieve a rush of euphoria from the next dopamine hit. We may go all out to feel good, only to experience fleeting moments of happiness before falling further into the bottomless pit of wanting more. The only remedy to this endless cycle of wanting more is to realize that we, as individuals, are enough.

I will be clear about what this book is, and what this book is not. This book is not about how to get rich quickly or how to become the next billionaire. There is nothing wrong with those goals, and if that's what you desire, then go for it. I'll be cheering for you every step of the way.

This book does not lay out the seven steps to achieve limitless prosperity, nor will this book unpack the secret to attracting the universal power of manifestation. I would much rather you identify your own strengths and talents, then build from there.

If that is what you are looking for, as of this writing, there are nearly half a million YouTube videos on such things. There are 100,000 such videos on wealth and 80,000 videos on "how to become rich." That information is out there, and it's out there in abundance. Yet here we are, still struggling to move the needle on generating and sustaining Black wealth. What are we missing?

My working theory is rooted in this idea of taking ownership of Black financial culture. I believe that Black financial culture is about choice and opportunity. It's about perspective and compassion. It is about grace and empowerment of others as well as self.

As an illustration of these things, I will share my personal journey without any strings attached or judgments made, solely for the purpose of offering a framework for your own progress. Whatever topics we delve into moving forward, please remember the following:

It's your money.

Do with it as you wish.

Just take some time to consider the outcomes of your choices.

Why *Black* Financial Culture? Simple. This book speaks to the spirit of what I believe to be true about Black people. Our ability to do a lot with a little is evident in the world around us, and yet, I want us to do more than survive. I want us to thrive. My military upbringing allowed me to enjoy a childhood full of diverse experiences. With that said, I appreciate and internalize the similitude of the Black experience. Our Black lives matter. Our Black health matters. Our Black relationships matter. Our Black communities matter. Our Black wealth matters.

Before we get the conversation started, I want to thank you for being open to a fresh, forward-thinking perspective on wealth creation. It's truly an honor and a privilege to contribute to such an important discussion, particularly during a critical moment for Black culture. My goal is for this book to serve as a valuable resource and guide for you, your loved ones, and your community for many years to come. Remember, you have more power than you realize, and it's time to embrace it!

With love,

Michael

2.
LESS SHAME. MORE EMPATHY.

I save because I remember my family's financial struggles during my childhood.

My mother was ensnared by bills.

I was nine or ten years old when I ran into my mother's bedroom, and she was surrounded by debt. Bills were sprawled across the bed, and her deliberation quickly turned into frustration.

I sat there, quietly, as she scribbled and scurried through the papers. After a few minutes, she pushed the statements away and pulled me in, tearfully.

"We are going to make it," she told me. "We are going to make it."

The *wolf at the door* is the language of living paycheck to paycheck. It is the stuff of pulpits and poverty. Some bills will get paid this month, some bills won't. It's a reality for many of us – the vicious cycle of robbing Peter to pay Paul.

That singular moment had a profound effect on my life. I didn't want to be a lion of a child, roaring for toys or trinkets. I wanted to be her peace, so I chose to be a lamb. I stopped asking for birthday and Christmas gifts. When the new school year rolled around, I didn't ask for new school clothes or shoes.

My mom always made it happen, but I felt her burden. So, if I ever asked for things, I was perfectly okay if the best we could manage was one outfit every few weeks from the local flea market.

That was tough on me during the hip-hop, basketball-driven nineties. Owning a pair of Jordans was a status symbol, which I failed to understand until I took my shot with one of the prettiest young ladies at my middle school.

"I think you're cute, but you don't dress well enough." The only thing that hurt worse than her words was the way she looked at my shoes. If "What are those?!?!" was a facial expression in the urban dictionary, it would have been her's in that moment.

My experiences as a child made me frugal – and fearful. My natural tendency to save works in overdrive because of trauma. The mere thought of lacking sufficient savings and having a spending plan makes me anxious, and I want to talk about how that ties into financial empathy.

Money, for the longest time, induced a sense of internal dread that took me back to some of the worst childhood memories. Here I was, a grown man, walking around with deeply seated financial tendencies that reflected where I once was and not who I had become. Unfortunately, we rarely discuss how our direct or indirect experiences with money, however young we might have been, can influence our relationship with our personal finances over a lifetime. Therefore, in order to develop a healthy relationship with money, we must be mindful of our financial past without guilt, shame or judgment.

This is why financial empathy is so important to a person's financial journey. Financial empathy is one's capacity to understand, feel, and respond with care to the context of another person's financial circumstances. This adds the invaluable component of compassion to Black financial culture.

Early in my career as a financial coach, I found myself focusing most of my time on my clients' numbers and what was financially optimal. Once I began operating from a place of dignifying instead of datafying the people I served, I started tapping into the higher levels of competent and compassionate care.

I once worked with a parent who did not want to submit her child's financial aid information for college. This was particularly perilous, because financial aid operates on a first-come, first-served basis. Despite the fact that her daughter was likely to be a recipient for federal grants, institutional aid, and other scholarships, she refused to cooperate.

A few people in my office erroneously concluded that neither the mother nor daughter cared about their financial well-being, and thus felt it was unnecessary to provide additional advice. They had considered the facts of the situation, but not the feelings of the people involved. The operative emotion was fear, and I empathized because of my lived experience. I didn't know the reason behind the family's actions, but I was convinced that there was a lot more to the story.

After three days of trying, I was able to reach the prospective student's mother by phone. Although I could sense her annoyance on the call, I intuitively knew it was fueled by fear rather than any personal animosity. Her daughter had an amazing opportunity sitting in front of her. I wasn't going to let this go. Black households tend to carry the highest student loan debt balances. A $35,000 student debt balance means that roughly $372 of future earnings will go towards paying off student loans. And nearly 85% of Black students are borrowing to attend college. Completing the FAFSA early, whether they chose to attend our college or not, was going to make a huge difference on the backend. You need cash flow to build wealth.

Initially, we didn't talk about financial aid. We talked about the mother's family and her day-to-day life. She talked about her struggles with working two jobs and how important her daughter was to her household, which included caring for her two siblings while her mother was away. As it turned out, the daughter was also apprehensive about leaving their family.

Fear manifests itself in different ways. My mom, surrounded by bills, relied on an optimism that rose from desperation. *We're going to make it.*

I internalized that situation as something to fear and became frugal, and it was that trauma which allowed me to feel this mother's pain. Instead of having them complete the process on their own, I scheduled some time to guide the two of them through the financial aid process and worked to find an institution closer to home. I also reassured them that our school would always be an option if they decided to change their mind. The family ended up processing their financial aid information in a timely fashion, which allowed the young lady to attend a college that was affordable and close to home.

For many of us, like my office mates, it is incredibly convenient to assume the worst about a person when we are unfamiliar with the context of their lives. Empathy doesn't live there. Neither does compassion. In fact, the opposite occurs. Prosocial shame, which is a way to enforce social sanctions as a way to promote desired behaviors. Yes, that's a thing. And it's very dangerous when said sanctions are derived from ignorance.

I've been shamed before. Maybe you have, too. I felt their judgment in the same way we tend to judge how people spend their tax refunds. Mind you, most people spend their tax refunds on credit card debt, medical bills, everyday living expenses, and an emergency reserve. This idea of prosocial shame reminds me of a story a friend once shared about the response of a tax preparer when a woman told him that she was going to buy a big flat screen television with her tax refund.

The tax preparer implored her to spend the money on something more sensible. The woman was not pleased with his tone or request. Even though they were both communicating in the language of money, they were approaching it from different vantage points.

"I live in a really rough neighborhood," she said. "If I buy this TV, I'll be able to keep my kids and their friends safe in our home, instead of them running around in the streets."

Financial rhetoric can bring the worst out of people because we only focus on the numbers, not humanity. Most people are trying to do the best they can with what they know, and embracing that reality is the beginning of empathy.

That reality is why I am a financial coach and educator. I attribute my ability to help people with their finances with the ability to unpack their *relationship* with their finances. Providing financial services is personal, relational, and technical. The best among us know how to navigate the space in the middle because money is not the main thing. (You're the main thing, remember?)

Meaningful connections to self, friends, family, and community are the true drivers towards financial success. Money is just a means to those ends. Empathy, not shame, is a much better vehicle to help people arrive at their desired destination. Acknowledging my own finance-related trauma helps me not just learn about my clients. I can actually see them – right where they are. No guilt. No shame. No judgment.

I believe when a person places judgment on someone else's financial decisions, it says more about the person placing judgment. A person's financial behaviors are likely byproducts of their experiences, but we would rather make assumptions that justify our beliefs and attitudes. This is more in line with one's capacity for sympathy. Sympathy is rooted in the familiar.

Empathy is an exploration, understanding, and respect for things that aren't.

By disguising it as "tough love," we shame individuals, but this approach is ineffective in the long run. It is important to acknowledge that our actions towards others not only impact their financial path but also our own, whether we choose to lean into shame or encouragement.

I believe empathy is the ultimate form of self-care because it leads to compassion for self and others. Developing this capacity does not happen overnight, though. Allow yourself the opportunity to grow by leaning into grace as we experience different seasons of growth, some sooner or later than others. Repeat this statement of mutuality with me:

I am right where I need to be.
They are right where they need to be.
I am being refined by my journey, not defined by it.
They are being refined by their journey, not defined by it.
Where I am does not dictate who I am.
Where they are does not dictate who they are.
It's not too late for all of us to experience financial wholeness and well-being.

Less shame. More grace. More empathy. More compassion.

I hope you feel the burden of judgment lift off your shoulders, and that your heart feels less heavy. Know that empathy is not a concession to bad financial habits, but a function of compassion. When we look past the numbers and look at the person, our sense of perspective, patience and persistence will manifest a culture of healing.

3.

SECURING THE BAG REQUIRES SECURING THE HEART

*How you spend money is a deep reflection
of what resides in your heart and soul.*

Let's take a moment for self-reflection. What are your spending habits? What are your saving habits? What is your internal self-talk when it comes to spending money? Actually, we can go further than that…

…Reflect on a time when you were young. What were your parents' or guardians' spending habits? What was the mood of your household on payday? Did that mood change when the bills came? Were your caregivers thrifty shoppers or did they have expensive tastes? Was money abundant? Scarce? Or a combination of both? How did you talk about money? What messages did you pick up? How did they make you feel? How do those experiences shape the way you think about and engage with money today?

If needed, now is a perfect time to put the book down, find a quiet space, and study you and your financial history by thoughtfully considering the questions I've presented. It's important because our financial decisions often stem from our upbringing and cultural influences. The early 2000s were filled with the lyrical musings of record labels named Cash Money. One particular song, "Still Fly" by Big Tymers, had a notably catchy chorus:

> *Gator boots, with the pimped-out Gucci suits*
> *Ain't got no job, but I stay shive*
> *Can't pay my rent, 'cause all my money's spent*
> *But that's OK, 'cause I'm still fly*

This was the language of extravagant spending, and I was caught up in the rapture for a brief stint. My student loan disbursement check dropped around the same time as "Still Fly," and that little slip of paper never stood a chance even though my spending was guilt-ridden every step of the way.

We can't remove Cash Money rhetoric from Black financial culture, even if respectability politics might turn up its nose in disapproval. Understand that pop culture can influence financial culture. Or, to think about it differently, hip hop was merely an echo of what was already the reality in the streets.

My mother, while not a hip-hop artist, shared the same rhetoric. "You might as well get what you want," she would say. "You can't take it with you."

Mom's spending was a coping mechanism, and it caused a number of financial ups and downs. My financial education on things like entrepreneurship, keeping track of my cash inflows and outflows, homeownership, saving and investing came from watching what worked and didn't work for her. She raised me during a time where life felt fleeting and unstable. Thus, you might as well enjoy what you can while you can.

This nature and nurture dynamic made me scared of money. My default mode of financial management was based on fear, not hopefulness, and I made a conscious choice to prioritize financial security over financial vulnerability. It was a joyless and unhealthy process for most of my adult years. I had very little life balance and felt anxious whenever I spent money for personal satisfaction. Even as I saved more money, I became increasingly guarded and apprehensive. I had learned how to secure the bag, but I failed to secure my heart in equal measure. As a result, even though I had more, I felt as if I had less and this overwhelming sensation that there was more to lose.

I found my peace in having an overflow of love. My wife's calming spirit and abundance mindset has been a godsend. I have gone to therapy to deal with my anxiety. I persevered through minor financial mishaps, which allowed me to gradually develop a perspective and adaptive response system that's become more self-secure.

When it comes to acquiring income and building wealth, I think about the words of Bruce Lee – "Be water, my friend."

Place your thumb at the end of a waterspout, and you'll make a mess of things trying to dam up the flow of water. Even in the presence of abundant water, there is no peace – only uncontrollable chaos.

A calm mind and a peaceful heart can allow money, like water, to flow abundantly to and from you. Water doesn't exist to simply nourish me. It exists to nourish all things that have the capacity to produce and sustain life.

Certainly, there are challenges to financial zen. I remember when my mom surrounded herself with all these pieces of papers with black due or red overdue dates, and I saw how frustrated she became in the face of debt. Bills can cause a fight or flight response, meaning that monthly billing statements can incite frustration, or make you so fearful that you don't even open your mail.

Maybe you're reading this book with skepticism. *Good financial advice can't save me. I'm in debt up to my eyeballs.* That voice is necessary. By allowing it to flow, without judgment or shame, we can determine the where and why of the chaos in the flow of our lives. The fact that you are reading this book despite everything you feel is a cause for celebration. You are disrupting unhealthy streams of thought for more productive ones.

Financial doubt isn't just a product of poverty or little resources. It can rise up in even the wealthiest of us. Another catchy hook from my teen years: "I don't know what they want from me/It's like the more money we come across/the more problems we see."

I don't think it was the late Notorious B.I.G.'s intent to scare people away from success or money. I think he spoke to the idea that money without wisdom can cause unnecessary complications. With that said, people have sabotaged their careers with the ideology of "Mo' Money, Mo' Problems."

I've worked with people who passed up amazing career opportunities because they feared that something bad might happen if their income grew above a certain level. It isn't a sin to be wealthy. In fact, money is morally neutral – not good or bad. Money can be a source of great joy once you learn how to set healthy boundaries and tend to it properly, but it also has the capacity to expose the contents of our heart. Which is why we have to be just as intentional about securing our hearts as we are in securing the bag.

I'm reminded of a quote from clergyman Norman Vincent Peale, who wrote a book about the power of positive thinking. "Empty pockets never held anyone back," he wrote. "Only empty heads and hearts can do that."

It is hard to manage and maintain money in the pursuit of aimless bag-chasing. Some of us have lost our way amid unrealistic expectations about success and life's endless distractions, while others have given up altogether in hopeless futility. Hopelessness tells us, "This is as good as it gets." But is it?

Put the book down for a moment and consider this: What's your endgame? Why are you working so tirelessly? Where will all of your efforts lead you? Is this really what you want? Why? Why is your why important to you?

I'm writing this book to help Black households develop a healthy and sustainable relationship with money. That's my why. My where, I would argue, is more important.

Your *where* is much deeper and should fuel your why. My where is rooted in the unshakable conviction that higher levels of financial well-being and economic agency lead to stronger families and more prosperous and loving communities. Money certainly matters, but is it a matter of our hearts? Maya Angelou put it this way: "At the end of the day people won't remember what you said or did, they will remember how you made them feel."

What does the pursuit of money drive within you? Is it an indicator of status or generosity? Is it a means of security or carefree living? The way you feel about money, whether positively or negatively, is a matter of your heart. And the Good Book tells us to guard your heart above all else, because everything you do flows from it.

I grew up in greater Gary, IN during a time when the area was often cited as the murder capital of the United States. I felt it was best to be as low key as humanly possible: low key in voice, posture, and visible displays of excess. I grew up in a neighborhood where you always had to be on high alert. We had been robbed. My mom had been mugged. I had friends who'd been jacked for cash, shoes, chains, watches, and sound systems from their cars. Outside of my tight-knit circle, I viewed most people skeptically, like Ice from *Paid in Full*.

Paid in Full, hands down, is one of my favorite movies. There aren't many movies I can watch more than once, but I have a few other favorites: *Shawshank Redemption, Malcolm X,*

Elf, Coming to America and the first *Home Alone* movie.

There's this one scene in *Paid in Full* where Mitch, one of the lead characters, is about to walk out of the corner shop. His uncle Ice, who happens to be there hanging out, challenges Mitch to provide more financial support to family members. Mitch replies, "I'm broke," while flashing some of his jewelry.

"I see you shinin', nigga," Ice responds. "I can smell a motherfucker with money. Even Ray Charles can see that you got money."

This scene is triggering for me and brings up so many negative emotions that I wrestle with about money. Just as sure as I was influenced by secular hip-hop songs, misquoted Bible verses about money being "the root of all evil" stuck with me. Having money made me feel like a target.

It wasn't until I sought therapy after a life-changing event in 2015 that I realized I had normalized my childhood trauma. Worse yet, I had allowed my early experiences to offset the financial gains I enjoyed in my adult life. Therapy created the space for me to unpack my core assumptions about the world and finances, and to reframe them in healthier and more productive ways. It changed my life.

You may be reading this and realizing that your relationship with money is a traumatic one. I want you to know that you are not alone in your realization. In order to heal, we must first reveal.

The revelatory process is tough. I scheduled therapy appointments, only to skip them because I rationalized my trauma. *There's nothing wrong with me. Man up. You're fine.* When I did attend sessions, I was reluctant to embrace the process due to fear of judgment, guilt, or shame. There was a pivotal moment during one of my sessions where my therapist reminded me about the difficulty of healing work. It won't be smooth or easy, but it will get better over time.

When we experience profound negative events in our lives, it rewires our brains. We create these new synapses and connections, which come with a permanent warning label. This is the birthplace of anxiety.

It will be very difficult to tap into abundance with a heart and mind full of fear. This is why we have to take our lives off autopilot and reassess the purpose in what we are doing.

Sometimes the optimal financial strategy has nothing to do with money. Just because you know better doesn't mean you'll do better. Don't you already know you should save? Invest? Have a life insurance policy? Limit the use of your credit card? You don't need me to tell you to do these things. Exploring *why* you aren't acting on what you know is where the real magic happens. If you know better but aren't doing better, it might be time to engage in the courageous task of unpacking your relationship with money in a way that allows you to see yourself with guiltless truth, self-compassion, and grace.

Before you secure the bag, you must first secure your heart. Therapy may be a viable solution that allows you to establish the emotional and psychological foundations to pursue, establish, and sustain your financial hopes and dreams.

4.

ABUNDANCE, ANYONE?

*Abundance is a decision before
it ever becomes a position.*

A few years ago, I picked up gardening in the spirit of "health is wealth." Since I've always loved blueberries, I went to the local farmers market and purchased two blueberry bushes. One was an early summer blooming plant, and the other bloomed later in the summer. It wasn't my intent to purchase both bushes, but the seller told me that without the other neither would bloom. Begrudgingly, I purchased both, even though I thought I was being hustled.

When my early summer blooming plant started to bud and produce small blueberries, I was on cloud nine. Before then, I debated whether or not I had inherited a green thumb from my grandmother, who was known for her proficiency in the garden.

A couple of weeks later, the berries began to plumpen, and I waited until the weekend to indulge in the *fruit* of my labor. (Dad joke!) That Saturday morning, I hopped out of bed like it was Christmas morning. Patience, not distance, made the heart grow fonder. When I stepped outside to pick my blueberries, I discovered that something or someone had already eaten them.

Birds? Other animals? Maybe a neighbor or one of the kids from across the way who is always in our yard? It didn't matter, everyone was a suspect. I even asked my wife if she had eaten my blueberries.

Then, out of nowhere, I experienced a calming thought. *You'll know you have abundance when the birds can pick from your bushes, and you still have enough left over to eat.*

If my subconscious had not spoken up, I would have gone into my default programming of scarcity instead of thinking abundantly. My immediate response would have been to vigilantly protect my two precious bushes. I might have detested anything and everything that might come near them, even my children. If I hadn't done therapy, I would have immediately lost my joy of gardening. A mindset of abundance, though, encouraged me to plant more blueberry bushes.

I didn't feel like I was being targeted or victimized because I invested in more "wealth" as my solution. Consequently, I haven't had any more issues with blueberry shortages – and neither have the birds.

That's the real essence of abundance. It's not a process of hoarding the things we own. Abundance is not a zero-sum game where someone has to lose in order for another person to win. That's scarcity. It is fearful, anxious, and unsure. Abundance, on the other hand, is confident and hopeful. Abundance says, "There is more where that came from."

Living through COVID-19 has been a test in abundance. For the first time in a long time, our emergency fund was going to be tested. We call it our "Get To" fund.

My wife and I chose that name because we didn't want to associate our past traumas with our current resources. We both experienced backgrounds where financial shocks meant going without lights, heat, or potential evictions. For the sake of our mental health, we needed to use language that was more about hopeful anticipation instead of one that induced a level of dread. We simply made the choice to change the labels on everything in life and our spending plan that no longer served us – even the way we thought and talked about money.

Our "Get To" fund ensured that an unexpected expense wouldn't thwart a family vacation or a financial milestone. Without that fund, the start of the pandemic could have hampered the plans we made. Despite my wife being temporarily unemployed, we were still able to do everything we had planned. We purchased a home and went on family vacations – in moderation, of course. We invested in the markets when they were down. We supported family and friends who needed help. We gave back to local Black businesses and other organizations. We even refinanced our home when the interest rates dropped to 2.5%. We executed the vision we set for ourselves when there were only rumblings of a potential Covid-19 outbreak. In other words, we still "got to" do everything we planned.

How did we do it? My wife and I decided to change our family culture around money several years ago. We adopted the mantra of "stay ready, so you don't have to get ready" in anticipation for obstacles or opportunities. There had been times when we weren't ready for an unexpected financial shock, and those times were tough on our marriage. Even as I write this, I can feel those instances still sitting in the pit of my stomach. We both agreed that we ain't doin' that again.

We also missed out on opportunities to connect with family and friends in addition to financially lucrative opportunities because we were strapped for cash. We decided to structure our lifestyle so that we lived on no more than 70 percent of our combined income, and thus, the "Get To" Fund was born.

We realized, in this case, that less meant more. Over an eight-year period, we acquired additional skills and established meaningful connections that were critical to increasing our earning potential. While my wife honed her abilities, I took care of everything else, and vice versa. We worked in this manner for a decade, which afforded us the opportunity to improve our income, pay off debt, and ramp up our savings. And I'll be completely honest with you, I don't how I could have done any of it without her and her without me.

Staying ready so you don't have to get ready means you must cultivate a culture of preparation for good times just as much as the not so good times. I recall the story of *Sports Illustrated* photographer Walter Iooss, Jr., the brilliant mind behind an iconic photo of Michael Jordan.

It's the photo where the GOAT, I said what I said, glided effortlessly through the air from the free throw line, midway between takeoff and an emphatic slam through the hoop. The way his feet are set up in the photo, he almost looks like another famous Michael, the King of Pop.

Iooss wasn't satisfied with his photos from the previous dunk contest in 1987 because people couldn't see the players' faces. He made key adjustments, which included a conversation with Jordan three hours before the dunk contest. He took the disappointment of his previous experiences, secured a better position during the slam dunk competition, and waited patiently to capture the moment. That moment turned out to be iconic. And came on the heels of a previous disappointment.

With preparation comes abundance, and the courage to grow in grace. I grew up in scarcity and had come to find comfort in it. I told myself that I didn't deserve more, that I might be corrupted by the influence of money. It was an attitude of fear, and even a little change in my pocket made me feel uneasy.

I still struggle with sharing my accomplishments because of my upbringing. Remember that house I told you that I purchased at the start of the pandemic? I only told three people about it initially. No social media posts. Nothing. I guess "Real G's move in silence like lasagna," Lil' Wayne rapped on "6 Foot, 7 Foot." But I was nothing close to a G. Visible display of wealth, still to this day, makes me feel uncomfortable.

That's an unfortunate commentary, because we should not live in fear or shame with abundance. The Good Book reveals that it is God's desire for us to live abundantly. Now, even if you don't believe in God, would you agree that having a positively expectant heart is a healthier way to live than expecting poverty to pounce on you like a thief in the night? Would you agree that being full of hope is better than being full of fear? Even if we don't agree about God, I think we can agree that abundant living is preferable, and that abundance doesn't always mean material possessions or money. Observe:

- You can have an abundance of peace, patience, and unyielding kindness.
- Joy and love can radiate abundantly in your spirit.
- Laughter and warmth can fill your home in abundance.
- Mental and emotional abundance can produce unalterable resilience.
- Being abundant in health and dexterity promotes longevity.

All of these descriptions have nothing to do with money. Abundance simply means to have an overflow of something. The last example mentions being abundantly healthy. If you lack good health, it can be very difficult to attain wealth because when you don't feel well, you're not at your best. If you're not at your best, your performance may suffer, which means you won't acquire the skills and relationships necessary to optimize your income throughout your lifetime. Conversely, let's say that you can amass wealth at the detriment of your health. Without good health, unfortunately, you won't have the capacity to enjoy all of your hard work in your later years. In either case, having an abundance of health matters for you, your family, and your community.

When was the last time you experienced an abundance of peace, love, joy, or health? Have you chased the bag so tirelessly that you have missed out on life's simple pleasures?

Chasing the bag can be a perilous lifestyle, and yet, it is one that society glorifies. We celebrate the tireless worker, and while society preaches balance, we rally behind the "work at all costs" mindset. Burnout is inevitable, and it's a story that repeats itself among the working class and rich folks alike.

Celebrity culture highlights the highs and hides the lows. Given that the public is unable to peek behind the curtain of famous people, it creates the illusion that money is the end-game. This culture trickles down to everyday people, who seek the quick but fleeting alternatives that produce unsustainable joy. We think that financial abundance, not holistic abundance, will fill the void of a broken spirit.

Here's the thing: it's not mo' money, mo' problems. It's mo' money, mo' options.

How we handle those options will determine whether we experience the joy and happiness we seek. Remember, money without wisdom is a liability. Without wisdom, more stuff only results in the triggering of a dopamine hit that produces momentary pleasure. Just like a sugary treat, once the sugar high is gone, we feel a strong desire to consume more, even to our detriment.

Again, balance is important. It's not one's intent to neglect self-care, family, friendship and community for money. It's cultural to think that money is a means to an end. Money, for many, is a conduit. Think of the word conduit like a channel through which something flows and connects two things. Social media is a conduit for staying up on the times, connecting with friends, and sharing important parts of our lives.

The Underground Railroad was a conduit of freedom, dignity, and the pursuit of the American dream for Black men, women, and children. This book is a conduit for building a new vision of Black financial culture that starts from the inside out. When one thinks of having an abundance of money as a conduit to a meaningful connection, we begin tapping into the real power of abundance, one that exists and thrives beyond ourselves. That type of mindset not only heals the individual, it is selfless in how it values others.

This brings us to a very critical point: **The Black community must consider viewing each other's success as a conduit for mutual benefit.**

Arguably the most familiar institution in the Black community is the church, and a common phrase that comes out of the church is "favor ain't fair." It suggests that the person who connects with religion will enjoy more success. I understand the intent of people saying they are "blessed and highly favored," but it can be individualistic at times.

Our faith should yield purpose, which then allows us to redistribute our blessings. My overflow is designed to be a blessing to others. Think about it this way — neither of my blueberry bushes would have bloomed without having the other to pollinate it. Now, you might bloom and produce fruit earlier than me. But neither of us would have the capacity to produce fruit without the other.

It's amazing, honestly. What I once saw as a hustle was a real-life parable about trust. I have been trusted with the overflow. Will I redistribute it or hoard it for myself? This is the difference between abundance and scarcity.

Perhaps abundance isn't practical in your current and unique position. I will tell you lovingly that abundance is a decision before it ever becomes a position. You must choose to think abundantly, despite past setbacks and any current obstacles you may face. You must live it before you live it.

Oh, it will be challenging, and yet someone has to be the catalyst for change. Someone in your family or community has to decide to be all in, to set the tempo for others who might follow. This is a tenet of leadership, and it resonates more when people see you doing things versus simply talking about them.

Therapy and a couple of blueberry bushes changed my life. This book is my testimony, because out of the abundance of the heart, the mouth speaks. My sincerest hope for you is a fullness that will change your life and the lives of those around you.

5.

GIVE ON
MY LEVEL

*What I give minus what I get is my
personal benchmark for wealth.*

This is a book about Black financial culture, which means that
there will be elements of Black culture in this book – hip-hop
and otherwise.

The songs I grew up on were so catchy. I can still hear the
thump that precludes the chorus of "Neva Eva" by Trillville and
Lil' Jon: "You can neva eva, neva eva … get on my level, get on
my level!"

I want us to have that level of energy and anticipation when
it comes to giving.

We should review our journey thus far. Therapy and healing
are instrumental in turning our lives around. This type of
reflection yields a mindset of abundance. It's hard to give in a
spirit of scarcity, and if one does, it rarely feels good. Above all
else, we should always be patient with ourselves. Mistakes will
be made along the way. They don't define you. Your commit-
ment to getting better – that's what defines you.

This review places us in a joyful state of mind. Joy is such
a powerful expression because it comes from within. It may
bend, but it doesn't break. It may expand, but it doesn't burst.

Joy isn't a fleeting emotion. It's an endless source of hope and an appropriate level of optimism regardless of our current circumstances. That's why we must prioritize things like healing, abundance, and self-compassion. Without them, giving has the capacity to drain us because we are giving from a well that is running dry.

Talking about joy in the face of trauma can be triggering. There are some people reading this who were children from abusive homes or who are currently living in abusive situations. To be clear, abuse can be physical or verbal.

There are other people reading this who have experienced unfathomable loss and are resorting to isolation instead of congregation. This is also a traumatic way to live, because no person is an island. "Out of sight, out of mind" doesn't cultivate strong emotional bonds, nor does it cultivate hopeful expectations.

"God loves a cheerful giver." This chapter, and honestly, my philosophy on finances, both derive from 2 Corinthians 9. Again, where we may disagree on religious preferences, we can agree that generous giving is vital in a healthy society. Conversely, a society absent of giving causes isolation and uncertainty. Regardless of your past circumstances, isolating yourself means limiting your capacity to be nurtured as well as becoming a nurturer.

Several years ago, I served as the director of admissions aid at a small liberal arts school in Georgia. One morning, my vice president wanted to meet with me. He wanted to help a young Black woman who made a profound impression on him and his family. They went out to eat one evening, and she provided joyous and excellent service at their table. As it turned out, she wanted to be a nurse, and on the way home from dinner, the entire family was compelled to make her dream a reality.

My vice president asked me to reach out to this young

woman. He wanted to gauge her interest in our institution and wanted to connect her with our financial aid office, nursing program, and other key members of the college.

While she couldn't attend our institution, her joyousness and service placed her within the proximity of a great opportunity. I had the chance to work with her briefly and learned of various challenges the young lady faced. Nevertheless, her joy never waned. She leaned into abundance and was full of self-compassion. Because she owned these characteristics, her joy was noticeable and contagious.

There is a familiar saying in our periodically downtrodden society – "hurt people hurt people." Now, replace hurt with the notion of service: Served people serve people.

There are so many ways to tap into the power of giving, whether it's serving an organization in the community, or helping someone in need. There are several studies that show how serving others can boost our mood, and improve our health and outlook on life. The same way "hurt people, hurt people," giving begets more giving.

Creating the space to generously serve others is a part of any introspective wealth creation strategy. Here's the secret sauce: muster enough courage to find opportunities to serve alongside people who don't always think or look like you. Just as diversification is important to investing, we must also diversify our social connections.

Diversity shouldn't be about tokenism or the status quo. It should uplift our differences while having appreciation for our similarities. Isolation can cultivate self-doubt or skepticism in people. Working alongside others can give you clarity of purpose and joy, and a sense of value and confidence that goes beyond anything that money can buy.

That said, I want to talk about the Black experience for a minute. Working alongside others can put us in the proximity of power, but what if you're already in a position of responsibility? How do you serve alongside the people in your own community?

We often talk about Blackness within the context of race, and rarely within the context of class struggles. Black people with moderate success can be hesitant to "help out the hood." Why? Because there are anti-Black elements in society that see Black folks as a threat rather than mutual partners. While in my youth, and because of the neighborhood I grew up in, to the outside world, I very rarely received the benefit of the doubt with regards to my character. I was a threat until proven otherwise. That type of thinking is unsavory and limits the untapped potential of countless individuals who are susceptible to internalizing and accepting the limitations that others place on them. Thank God I had a mother who told me as often as she could, "You are somebody."

Giving doesn't always have to be a monetary endeavor. "Everybody can be great because everyone can serve," Martin Luther King Jr. once said.

You and I were placed on this earth to be of benefit to each other. Let us share our gifts generously. Otherwise, my capacity to give at an even higher level is limited because I have yet to be blessed by the full magnitude of the joyful impact you are destined to make on this earth.

I need you! We need you!

6.

LIVE YOUR LEGACY!

Every legacy requires someone to run the
first leg of the race. Why not you?

I've told you so much about myself and my mother. Now, it's time to tell you about my sister, Tiara.

She was always my protector and biggest supporter. There would be no Michael Thomas slander in her presence. She was a southpaw who would put them paws on you if you said anything about her big brother.

Our childhood was rocky and unsure at times despite my mom trying to hold it all together, but she was my rock. As Tiara grew from being my little sister to a compassionate and fearless woman, she represented this type of foundation for many others. She would do anything for family, friends, and acquaintances, money be damned. She planned birthday parties, sleepovers and special events for other people's kids. She would help pay other people's bills and cosign on loans with which she felt comfortable. She was a sure thing – a real nurturer.

I miss my sister.

November 18, 2015. Two weeks before, Tiara sent out invitations to her bridal party. A week before, she and I talked about her pending graduation from college and Thanksgiving plans. She wanted me to bake an apple pie.

I miss my sister.

November 18, 2015. My sister was murdered – shot to death by her ex-boyfriend and father of their three children, who were 11, 8 and 5 at the time. The night she was murdered, she made a Facebook post about seafood and seeing her fiance. Crab legs. A delicacy, just like life. And just as frail.

I received the news en route to Jacksonville for a financial planning conference.

I was scheduled to present a poster on the impact that fatherlessness has on the financial well-being of children. Never in a million years would I have considered the impact that motherlessness has on a child, and certainly not the impact it might have on my niece and nephews.

I thought I knew grief. I was wrong. God, I hope no one ever receives that type of phone call. I was so angry, so sad, so burdened. I felt as free as a bird before that call, only to have my wings violently snatched off.

Tiara was my source of strength and confidence in adulthood, just as she was during our childhood. She's the one who told me she had no doubt that I could be a Ph.D., when I nearly backed out of the program. Scarcity suggested that I was just a kid fortunate enough to make it out of Gary, and that was enough. Tiara wouldn't stand for it, and if I didn't listen, I'd have to see those hands.

How would I exist without her constant reassurance? I was lost. My family was lost. A whole community was lost. And then, the stories rolled in.

Tiara is the name of a regal woman's crown. It is the picture of prestige and legacy. The week before Tiara's funeral, my entire family received an overwhelming amount of support. While my mother, a few others and I finalized funeral arrangements, the legend of my sister was told through various anecdotes.

People told stories of her fortitude, of her motivational tactics. They talked about how she loved them when they needed it the most. As a nurturer, she had the ability to see beyond people's self-doubts and instead focus on their potential to become something more.

I received message after message about good deeds that never saw the light of day, good deeds that never expected anything in return. I knew my sister was an amazing person in my life, but I never knew she was an amazing person to so many others. Selfishly, I thought that she was only my rock, a secret weapon to employ against my negative mindset. Nah. Tiara loved people even when it was inconvenient. She wore her crown and lived her legacy. I can still hear her saying, "It's OK. Choose to love anyway."

I couldn't. I wanted blood. How could someone do this to my little sister? For years, I wanted to avenge her death. But I continued to hear her voice.

I grew stronger in my conviction to live for Tiara and honor her legacy. If her legacy lived, so did she. This mindset took me through some of the darkest times of my life. I was deeply depressed and had nightmares, which resulted from post traumatic stress disorder. Almost a year and a half after her murder, I relived and reenacted that tragedy each morning before I woke up. My efforts to comprehend it proved to be fruitless. For another year and half beyond that, I didn't want to feel anything or embrace the light of day. I just wanted to be alone and completely embrace the darkness that was consuming me.

Little did I know, Tiara's legacy, not her tragedy, led me down a path of forgiveness. As I write about empathy, about being a light amid darkness, I am telling you from a very raw place of personal experiences. I'm sharing my story to illustrate the importance of your character and its impact on others.

Your legacy is what you live so that you can have a clearer vision of what you wish to leave and how you wish to leave it. In essence, with thoughtfulness and careful planning, you can live well beyond your time here on earth.

Legacy isn't just a matter of the metaphysical, though. It's also very functional.

Three months prior to Tiara's passing, we discussed her need for life insurance and a will. She told me that she thought about it and promised to look into it. I took her word for it and didn't bring it up again.

After working through her financial affairs, it became clear that she didn't have life insurance or a will. Our family, with my mom leading the charge, her strength and resilience is beyond admirable, pulled together resources to bury Tiara and to provide some ongoing support for my beautiful niece and amazing nephews. It wasn't until eight years later that I learned that Tiara had indeed scheduled an appointment to purchase life insurance. She was on the schedule to see the life insurance agent that upcoming Friday. They had rescheduled their initial meeting that was set for the week before.

Since the pandemic, the percentage of Black families who have purchased life insurance has gone up significantly. However, the process isn't just about getting life insurance as a significant number of Black households allow their life insurance policies to lapse. It's also about maintaining life insurance coverage. I want to use this dynamic, within the context of legacy, to ask you a few questions.

- How are you currently living the legacy that you wish to leave?
- Clearly define what your legacy means to you using the three "Whys?" approach:
  - Why is your legacy important to you?

- Why is your response to the first response important to you?
- Why is the response to the second question important to you?
- What have you done to protect your legacy and ensure that it lives beyond you?

Being able to pass along your estate – money and property – to your children, family, friends and organizations you support is only a part of the process. Your estate has a higher purpose. It should serve as a conduit towards expanding upon your legacy – your faith and your works. Your character, not your money, is the **REAL** legacy. With that being said, establish a clear vision for what you hope to pass along to your heirs, because money alone may not be enough. In fact, nearly 70 percent of heirs blow through the money they have inherited within one generation. That's generational wealth depletion, not generational wealth creation.

Morals and wisdom often have a longer shelf life than money. Creating the foundation of those things, along with money, is the real flex. If trauma can pass from generation to generation, so can wholeness.

Tiara's death was tragic, to say the least. Her unconditional love, which inspired me, has been passed down to her children through the resilience and unfailing love of our grieving mother. I don't know how she held it together. But she did. She always does. As a result, generosity is the vehicle we use to reflect her legacy. It's how we choose to live with purpose and intention. Her spirit will live forever through our actions. When you picture it this way, I think you might find it easier to see the joy and beauty in the process of establishing a will and adequate life insurance to support, facilitate, and protect your legacy.

Let's break this down a step further. We support our legacy by ensuring we have the financial resources to execute the vision of our legacy. For instance, one of the many visions for my legacy is to ensure my family maintains a certain standard of living in the event something happens to me. I want them to be able to afford memorable travel experiences, have access to quality education, and live in a community of people who share our values. I want to ensure my wife has the financial support she needs and that my boys don't have to worry about college expenses or a down payment on their first home. While I am working on these goals during my time on this earth, life insurance is a great way to provide the financial support that accompanies the vision. My sincere hope is that my wife and boys will have the space to heal and strength to prioritize generosity to honor my legacy.

If you don't currently have life insurance, there are several types on the market. I won't unpack all of them here. I want to simplify the process so that you get around to doing the thing you might be putting off. At the very least, consider a term policy – meaning that you can receive affordable life insurance coverage for a term (for example, 10, 15, 20, or 30 years). The shorter the term, the less expensive the policy. So, if you are trying to get your finances in order, there is likely a term life insurance policy that matches your needs. A quick Google search will help you find and compare the most affordable policies available to you.

You can estimate your insurance coverage in a couple of ways:

- Consider how much you can afford on a monthly basis. I call this the baseline approach. List what you can afford to pay on a monthly basis on a term life insurance platform and the system will let you know what you qualify for in term life insurance. Remember, **getting an insurance policy that you can financially sustain is just as important as getting insurance.** Unfortunately, many families take on costly policies that they allow to lapse. And that doesn't do anyone any good.

- The second approach to consider is the multiplier approach. You take your annual income and multiply it by ten. Let's say that you earn $45,000 a year. Multiply it by 10 (for example, $45,000 x 10 = $450,000). The number you calculate will be the insurance policy amount you should consider. If the monthly payment for this amount of coverage is unaffordable, divide the policy amount you just calculated by two (for example, $450,000 / 2 = $225,000) and consider starting your insurance coverage there. At the end of the day, it's not just about getting insurance coverage, it's also about being able to keep the insurance coverage you get.

After you've established your insurance coverage, you will need to identify your beneficiary(ies). This is a very important and perpetual aspect of securing your legacy. Some people don't complete the process. Others will have an outdated beneficiary or make young children the beneficiaries of their life insurance policies. Did you know that insurance payouts cannot be paid directly to a minor? Instead, that money goes to the caregiver of the minor(s), who serves as a custodian of those resources. Although it is the custodian's responsibility to manage those resources for the child, I've seen way too many households blow through those resources, leaving the children with nothing when they become adults.

Consequently, it isn't enough to get a financially sustainable insurance policy. You will also need to consider who among your friends and family should be entrusted with your kids and your money. Otherwise, the state will decide through a process known as probate. Establishing a will says that you know your friends and family better than the courts. Again, money without wisdom is a liability.

Remember being 18 years old? Maybe you're 18 now. Do you trust yourself with a million dollars? Most of us would not be able to handle that amount of money under normal circumstances. Now, consider how much more difficult it would be to make objective financial decisions after experiencing the grief that comes with losing a loved one. Honestly, I wouldn't trust myself right now under those conditions and I'm good with money.

Moreover, what do Takeoff, Chadwick Boseman, Prince Rogers Nelson, John Singleton, Aretha Franklin, and Michael Jackson all have in common? They all passed away without a will. Sadly, they did not clearly define who would have the responsibility of settling the affairs of their estate – an executor.

An executor is a person who carries out the last wishes, or the legacy, of the deceased. Dying without a will can transform a mourning family's grief into greed. Folks end up fighting over money instead of cherishing memories and executing the vision of the loved one. Here are a few things to consider:

- How do I want my legacy to live beyond me?
- Do I need a **trust and trustee** to ensure that my estate is used for those intentions?
- Who can I entrust to ensure my legacy lives beyond me? Who will be my **executor?**
- If I was incapacitated or unable to make decisions for myself, who would be my **power of attorney** – a person designated to act on my behalf?
- Who would be in charge of making vital life or death decisions – **healthcare proxy** – about your health?
- If you already know the types of decisions you would

like to make regarding your health, has that been communicated through an **advanced directive?**

- Who will be the **legal guardian** of perhaps your most precious assets, your children and pet(s), if something were to happen to you?
- When establishing my will, do I know enough about my state's laws to ensure that it will stand in the court of law? If not, who within my social networks can help me find an estate attorney to help draft my will? Are there pro bono or free services for this in your area?

The beauty in all of this is that you get to decide. You get to ensure that your legacy lives on for generations. My sister, although well-intentioned, kept putting off securing the financial aspects of her legacy. Luckily, my amazing mother was willing to step in and love on her babies the way Tiara would have. Some people are not that lucky. For some, family members don't step up and everything is left to the system, which can provide unfortunate outcomes.

This does not have to be you, or any of us. Securing the bag and our hearts is only part of the process. We must be intentional about securing our legacies through affordable life insurance and professionally executed wills.

I know this is a heavy discussion. Lord knows I think about Tiara every day. Organization and vision are keys to legacy. Take a step back from your hectic life. Lean into your strengths and create a system that works best for you. Many people struggle with establishing a will because it means that they have to be intentional about gaining real clarity around their finances (liquid cash, investments, property, business dealings, etc.) and relationships.

Let's be honest. The process can be overwhelming. However, if you break each task down into small manageable pieces and extend yourself some grace along the way, you'll start to feel better about the process and more confident about securing your future.

Furthermore, you'll be setting a positive example for your household and community on how and why it's important to take care of these things. It's okay to start slowly. This means that once you've finished, you'll be confident enough to help others navigate the technical, organizational and emotional aspects of the process.

7.

NO MORE "WALL" STREETS

*Forgiveness is a financial wellness
and wealth creation strategy.*

"Wall Street" is a term synonymous with finance. It quite literally is the financial center of our country, and at times, the world. Certainly, someone with a vested interest in finance and investment related matters would speak glowingly of Wall Street.

For the rest of us, not so much.

Wall Street often feels cold, apathetic, divisive. Walls, in and of themselves, are dividers, which can speak to the barrier(s) between the haves and the have-nots. It wasn't too long ago that *Occupy Wall Street* was a thing. For 59 days, thousands of protestors used this opportunity to speak out against the economic inequality experienced on main street.

Oftentimes, political leaders will make decisions for the "good of our economy." Those decisions often come at the expense of working-class people as Wall Street's chief aim is to drive corporate profits.

Wall Street is also Black financial culture. Black folks built Wall Street, albeit, not of our own free will. Our men, women, and children were bought and sold on Wall Street. Black people built the original wall for which the street is named, a barrier designated for protection from England.

About walls. Sure, walls can provide protection from known and unknown threats. They can also stifle our growth and the spirit of community. Throughout human history, walls have been established for various reasons and with mixed public sentiment. The Great Wall of China. The Berlin Wall. The calls in the United States to "build the wall."

A strong wall doesn't just keep stuff out. It keeps us in. What is impenetrable can also be inescapable – a prison of our own making.

Perhaps we should look at relationships. Have you ever put up walls that prevent communication? Did the walls that someone else put up make you hesitant to trust them? Walls, for what they offer in protection, also harbor insecurities.

A few years ago, I received news that an old neighbor of mine had a terminal illness. Even though my family and I had moved hundreds of miles away, I felt compelled to visit him. Mr. Eddie was an older, happily married gentleman, usually upbeat. He always knew the news of the neighborhood, kind of like Kim Wayans' character on *In Living Color.* He wasn't one to gossip, though.

When we last spoke, Mr. Eddie fussed at me because I never wore a hat while I mowed the lawn. Even though he lived three houses down, he always made his presence felt. *Mike, now, I ain't gonna tell you again. You need to keep somethin' on your head. You young now. But you gonna be old like me someday.*

Somehow that conversation led to us hanging out and drinking a couple of cold ones. We talked about everything under the sun. It had been several years since I had last seen him, but I wanted to give him his roses while he was still alive. I wasn't afforded the same opportunity with my sister.

Unfortunately, our reunion did not go as I had expected.

Mr. Eddie, now about 40 pounds lighter, lived alone and drank heavily. When I arrived unexpectedly and knocked on his door, he grumpily yelled, "Who in the hell is it?... Mike, is that you?"

He warmed up a little, but not much. I sensed that while he was glad to see me, he didn't want me to see him in this condition. Reluctantly, he invited me in and acknowledged my hat. "I see you finally learned to listen," he said.

For the next two hours, we sat on his front porch and talked about his frustration with his illness, struggles with faith, the separation between him and his wife, and the lack of support he received from his children. Mr. Eddie was bitter. He was so upset that he canceled his insurance policies and changed all the beneficiaries on any money he had for investments.

"Those motherfuckers ain't gettin' nothin' from me," he repeated time and time again. I can still hear the resentment dripping from his words.

Months later, I was informed that Mr. Eddie had passed away. He and his wife never reconciled, and he stopped communicating with his children. He died alone. I felt a great deal of pain from his death, but I felt greater sorrow because of the brokenness he took to his grave. His last days were walled off from the rest of the world. No community. No meaningful connection. Isolation and bitterness consumed him. Worse yet, someone reading this, maybe you, has been hurt so profoundly that the walls are up, and they ain't comin' down – at least no time soon. And, like Mr. Eddie, although you created those walls to protect yourself, they also prevent you from releasing the pain and suffering you feel.

Perhaps you're reading this chapter and realize that you have intense emotions that prevent you from feeling the pain and suffering of others. You can't fathom compassion. You're numb. I don't know about your pain specifically and the context behind it. In fact, I'll never know it the way you do. But I do understand that your emotions from betrayal, hurt, disappointment and suffering are real.

"Hurt people, hurt people," isn't always a deliberate dynamic. Sometimes that hurt is inadvertent. Still, the spirit of scarcity is prevalent. It is dangerous to operate from the perspective that someone must lose for us to win. Walls perpetuate a "me versus them" mindset, and we lose our ability to feel anything outside of ourselves.

We become slaves to our own emotions, never realizing the binding power of our deep, unresolved wounds. If these walls could talk, what would they say about our inability to trust and to profoundly love others?

A lack of trust is the precursor to the downfall of relationships. And many of us have found ourselves on the receiving end of betrayal. So why, then, would we engage in any process that could benefit others? Why would we establish insurance policies and go through a time-consuming estate planning process to secure a better tomorrow for our kinfolk? Why would we save for the future and invest in helping future generations? No one was there for you in your time of need. No one left you an inheritance. No one cares about your well-being: emotional, financial or otherwise. I've personally witnessed how unresolved bitterness can wreak financial havoc in an individual's personal and financial life. Worse yet, the devastation can become generational and create blockages like the pungent smell of stagnant pools of water.

Water was not designed to be stagnant or walled off. It was designed to flow, hence the word current. I feel the same way about human beings, about money – currency. Sadly, many of us have walled off our sense of well-being. The solution from damming up our legacies is forgiveness. Dammit, I said it. Forgiveness!

Black folks are the most forgiving people. Why is that a bad thing? We must unpack what forgiveness is and how it benefits us. Forgiveness is letting go of the emotional weight of the past to embrace the possibilities that currently exist. Forgiveness does not mean that you must forget or ignore the sting from past slights or injustices. It's quite the opposite. Forgiveness allows us to be refined by our experiences, not defined by them. Forgiveness has the power to bring the walls down so we can embrace the currency of trust and, as a result, unlimited opportunities. You can't heal what you don't reveal.

When I lost my sister, my walls went up. I didn't want to feel anything. I didn't want to strive for anything. My life felt pointless for the better part of two years. I was just as bitter and angry as Mr. Eddie.

I had suicidal thoughts. My apathy yielded a 60-pound weight gain, and I drank heavily. My saving habits went to pot. I walled my heart off from everyone.

So, what changed? I confronted God.

Faith is foundational in my life. It helps me make sense of the world. Tiara's death just didn't make sense, though. I wrestled with God, cussed him out, punched walls. I purged what felt like a bottomless rage. I was going downhill fast. Something had to change. So, I did what I always do. I got back to my word.

In fact, I lost myself in scripture, sometimes full of resentment. The stories where Jesus demonstrated forgiveness triggered me. Nevertheless, I sat with those stories for months.

I was angry with God, but I was angrier with Kevin. He was my brother, the father of Tiara's children. He murdered my sister, just before her dreams could become reality.

It took a long time for me to forgive Kevin. But the forgiveness process started when I embraced my grief independent of rage. I realized that Kevin was not beyond God's grace and mercy. Kevin was not beyond redemption.

I was Joshua in the battle of Jericho, and the walls came tumbling down. I crumbled as well, in a heap of tears – and hope.

People still can't believe that I've forgiven Kevin, and I've shared my testimony to puzzled looks. I understand that my sense of forgiveness is peculiar, but this is my path forward. This is my faith on full display.

If hurt people hurt people, then healed people heal people. And if healed people heal people, there is a massive opportunity to create roaring currents of trust and currency in the Black community, which can create lasting ripples for generations to come. Wealth without wholeness is nothingness, and healing happens through forgiveness of self and others.

Making amends is a personal choice, and I'm only sharing my testimony. I often think about how people interpret my sense of forgiveness and think back to the old me. The thought of forgiveness made me feel weak. It felt as if I was disrespecting my sister and her legacy. But when I decided to choose forgiveness, I soon realized that it was the very thing that rekindled the spirit to choose love even when it's inconvenient.

8.

IN*VEST

Wealth begins with we, not I.

What is wealth? It's a calculation. Subtract your liabilities, or debts you owe, from the fair market value of your assets. Fair market value is the amount a reasonable buyer would pay for an item you own. And there you have it – your wealth position.

Let's say someone you know has $700,000 in assets – the items you own that have value – and $1 million worth of debt. That person's wealth position would be **negative $300,000** ($700,000 - $1,000,000). This means that they have more debts than assets. On the other hand, another person you know may "only" have $150,000 worth of assets and no debt. Their wealth position is **positive $150,000.** They have more assets than liabilities.

Wealth is a calculation, not a perception. Regardless of what you see on social media or mass media, you cannot determine someone's level of wealth without looking at their numbers. Considering that many people do not maintain a spending plan, track their debt, value their assets, and monitor and update their wealth position, it stands to reason that most people aren't sure about their *own* wealth calculation.

Take a few minutes to answer the following questions:

- How much money do you earn each month (including found money, gifted money, side job, etc.)?
- What is coming out of your check (taxes and other items)? Are you contributing too much or too little in these areas? How do you know?
- Where does all your money go each month after you get paid? How much are you spending in each of those categories?
- If you have debt, how much do you owe? What are your interest rates? How much of your income is being eaten up by monthly debt payments? What types of debts do you owe? Do the items that you are paying for on a monthly basis still bring you joy? Are they a burden?
- What assets do you own? What is the fair market value of those assets? Are they appreciating or depreciating in value? When you consider your assets in relation to your debt, what is your wealth position?

Were you able to answer all of those questions? I hope so. Were you able to answer them in a timely fashion? Financial data suggests that the answer is no as most people prefer not to think about money. Not being able to answer all of the questions or being able to do so quickly is perfectly fine. You are venturing down the path of wisdom, which is the *application* of knowledge. And money without wisdom is a liability.

I keep the answers to the above financial questions in a secured spreadsheet. It's that simple – for myself and my family. In the event that something happens to me, not only do we have our affairs in order, but my wife and children can find and access any pertinent financial information about me. Now, here's where things get interesting. Send those same questions in a group chat to family and friends. This is what I like to call a **Financial Fire Drill.** As with money, the best way to navigate a fire is proactive preparation, not reactive desperation.

I believe there are too many people who find comfort in the illusion of movement. Just because someone appears to be moving doesn't mean they are making meaningful progress towards a worthy goal. Just like running around frantically with your clothes on fire won't put it out.

How many people do you know, yourself included, who have imagined big plans? Maybe they want to start a business, write a book, or get their finances in order. Folks will talk about their plans for hours, then leave the conversation feeling a sense of accomplishment. Months later, their plans are still at square one. Years later, their plans are still at square one! That's the illusion of movement – getting lost in the framework of our plans and not the actual work of building them.

I taught my oldest son the proper way to do push-ups a few years ago. First, I wanted to see his interpretation, and he rattled off 18 sad-looking push-ups. He popped off the floor and yelled, "I'm a man!"

I looked at him and might have even side-eyed him. I corrected his form and instructed him. He needed to steady himself and his chest had to hit the floor.

"You got that, son?"

"Yep. I'm a man!"

I showed him the framework, but he still needed to do the work.

He only completed four push-ups the second time around, and immediately wanted to go back to his old framework. Why? "Because I'm able to do more push-ups that way." The illusion of movement was more important to him than actually building a firm foundation of strength.

Flash versus substance. Keeping up with the Joneses. Those sayings fall under the same umbrella, and many of us fall victim to it. I want us to move with integrity, because this is the start of investing.

In 1785, Robert Burns wrote the following: "The best laid plans of mice and men often go awry." Even the most well-calculated strategy can lead to failure. If this is the case, what chance does a person have who "makes moves" only for social acceptance with no organization? What chance does a person who has accumulated consumer debt have in keeping up with the Joneses?

Certainly, there is nothing wrong with social acceptance, and social capital carries significant value. The challenge many face is that we desire the form of success without the substance – without the investment.

The ways we spend our time, energy and money are important. Before you fully embrace the process of securing the bag through investing, it is important that you establish the appropriate foundation. Otherwise, you'll fall into the trap of trying to do the right thing with bad information at the wrong place and at the worst possible time and call it progress.

In. Vest. In. Vest. In. Vest. Most of us hear the word "vest" and think about clothing. "Vest" is also the act of conferring or bestowing power. Where are you channeling your resources, energy and power?

That said, I love to invest. Why? It inspires good habits. When I invest, I eat out less. Therefore, I conclude that investing is good for my health. Another important reason is that the process of investing challenges me to grow. When I grow through reading, mentorship, and trial and error, my money tends to follow suit.

Suit. Ahhh…There goes that whole clothes theme again. The word "invest" comes from the Latin word "investir," which means to clothe. "In," when used as an adjective, means to orient the direction of something inward. "Vest" means to place authority or power with someone or something. **The way I see it, the foundation of investing is the process of clothing my internal self with worth, value, and power so that I can transfer it in a way that produces greater value, worth, and power.** Clearly, investing starts within me and you.

Sometimes it has to start with the individual. Sometimes no one else is willing. Sometimes no one else has the capacity to take courage and tap into their power. Someone must be the spark to ignite the ignition. Speaking of which, several years ago, I was home for the summer after my freshman year in college. I was posted up in Mom's room waiting for her to get home from work. Her bedroom sat right over the garage, so I knew whenever she pulled up to the house. Normally, I had a general idea of when Mom arrived, but for some reason, she was later than usual. I fell asleep.

Then, out of nowhere, a frantic voice wrested me from my slumber. "MICHAEL!"

It was my mom. Two individuals tried to mug her and grab her purse. I ran down the stairs with the first weapon at my disposal – a baseball bat. One of our neighbors turned on her lights, which deterred the muggers.

Everything within me wanted to pull up on the first two people I saw that night, regardless of who they were. Mom, who was noticeably shaken, held me back. And I am glad that she did. I was going to do all of this with a baseball bat when they could have been armed. We quickly called the police instead.

The police did not arrive quickly, however. They showed up 45 minutes later.

I was frustrated as hell, and because it was dark, Mom didn't get a good look at the muggers. The cops left. I didn't sleep at all that night.

The next day, our neighbor mentioned a string of robberies that had occurred over the last week, just within a few blocks of our home. "Why aren't we talking about this as a community?" I thought. "We're just gonna keep letting this shit happen and not do anything about it?"

I refused to let it slide. I created and left flyers at people's homes. I talked to neighbors about what happened to my mother. I had to do something. Why? Because no one else stepped up – not my neighbors, not the police. It was at that moment that I realized no one was coming to save me. I had to do that for myself.

A movement can start with one person. You are the person who can change the destiny of your family and your community. Believe in yourself. Invest in yourself.

But it is also important to be gentle with yourself.

We often mention forgiveness in terms of other people. We should forgive ourselves, also. Sometimes, we spend so much time seeking externally what can only be found internally. Your past should refine you, not define you. Forgive yourself. Afford yourself the opportunity to view the past without judgment and shame. You are worth the investment.

Wealth is a calculation, not a perception. Forgiveness, however, is a perception. It's a way of looking at the world in such a way that breaks down walls and restores relationships. It cultivates sustainable wealth, which can change the fortunes of Black people and Black financial culture.

We celebrate Black wealth through the lens of individuals, not as a collective. This is a dynamic that must change, because wealth begins with, WE, not I. Although this process may begin with you, it won't end with you. It's going to take all of us, as a collective, doing what we can to move the needle on wealth in the Black community.

One study found that roughly 50 percent of Black households

are not invested in the stock market, and that nearly 60 percent of Black women aren't invested in any assets. Our lack of participation in the investment markets has prevented us from making significant strides to improve our wealth position. I get it. Without a foundation of trust within ourselves, families, communities, and the bedrock of our nation, it's a bit of a stretch to trust the markets. So, at the very least, let's talk about it.

The Standard and Poor's 500, or simply the S&P 500, is a stock market index tracking the stock performance of 500 large companies listed on stock exchanges in the United States. It is broadly considered the best measurement of U.S. market activity. The diversification that exists within this basket of companies lowers the types of risk we can control considerably. Think of it this way. If you are invested in one company and it goes out of business, you've lost your entire investment. When you invest in a diversified portfolio, you are only exposed to a little risk across all the companies. In the event one company fails, you may not feel it because you might have another company, or several, you've invested in to make up for those losses. That's the power of diversification and the beauty of the S&P 500 index.

Moreover, companies don't just fall within the S&P 500 index. A committee of experts meets quarterly to assess the companies held in the index. If there are companies that appear to be on a downward trajectory or companies that have demonstrated stellar performance over a period, this committee will make changes to its company holdings as needed. This, in short, is one less thing you'd have to worry about as an investor.

The average annual return from 2008 to 2022 in the S&P 500 was 9.5 percent, which includes the Great Recession (housing market collapse and high unemployment) and the pandemic years (lockdowns and inflation). Historically, the average return of the stock market is 10 percent. Despite two major financial shocks within close to a decade's time, the average return has fared well. Yes, there was volatility. However, this means that while some companies didn't do well during that time, others did. Hence, the importance of spreading one's investments – even when we are convinced that we have an absolute winner.

An average annual return of 9.5 percent may not seem like a lot, but it's a big deal. Let's do some quick math. The 2020 U.S. Census reported there are roughly 41 million Black people in the U.S. If half the Black population is not investing, that means roughly 20.5 million people have zero involvement with the stock markets. What does that mean in the context of a 9.5 percent return? How does Usher say it? Watch this.

If one of the 20.5 million Black non-investors collectively saved $40 a month ($10 a week) in a savings account, earning no interest, from 2008 to 2022, the value of those savings would be $6,720. The collective value of those savings, not considering the corrosive nature of inflation, would be $138 billion. That's a lot of money!

If those same savings were invested and grew at the average rate of return of 9.5 percent for that same time period, the collective Black wealth would have grown to – watch this! – $286 billion by letting the markets do the work. Those returns would continue to grow exponentially in value if left untouched.

We have not yet considered the other half of Black individuals who are already investing in stocks as well as those who own businesses, real estate, collectibles, etc. One report estimated that collective Black wealth as of 2020 was close to $5 trillion, which is $98 trillion less than White households. Despite this disparity, encouraging higher rates of stock market participation along with sustainable homeownership and entrepreneurship are the surest path towards wealth creation by adopting a wealth creation state of mind.

Some might consider it impossible, but if poverty can be generational, why can't prosperity? I see it as physics – for every action, there is an equal and opposite reaction. One possibility cannot exist without the presence of the other. If the Black experience has been historically mired in extreme misfortune, this would suggest to me that we are due for unfathomable fortune. But we'll never strive for this type of outcome unless we can see the opportunity within us first.

One person's actions can have an extraordinary ripple effect on their family, community, and culture, particularly in the context of Black financial culture. After knocking on hundreds of doors when my mom got mugged, I realized that people did care. They wanted to do more. They just needed to know that other people cared, too. That experience reminds me of one of my favorite African proverbs: "If you want to go fast, go alone. If you want to go far, go together."

Moving the wealth needle for Black households means we must prioritize inter- (within) and intra- (between) family wealth creation as a part of THE culture. In the illustration above, $6,720 saved didn't seem like much, but when you view those individual efforts as a collective, it's a sight for sore eyes.

I understand the challenges more than you know. But I did not make it this far in life focusing on my obstacles. I got this far because I became obsessed with the opportunities that lay ahead. We can't change the past, but we can commit to seizing every small moment, one moment at a time.

Despite all that we've experienced throughout our history, we are more resilient and better prepared to create a collective bounty greater than what we can conceive is possible. Financial empathy, self-compassion and forgiveness aren't just buzzwords or mental health mumbo-jumbo in this process. They are the investments we must make to yield the returns we seek.

Most of us avoid important financial conversations until

someone dies, and then we discover our loved one didn't have life insurance or a will. We avoid those conversations until Mom and Dad call one day, letting us know they have nothing saved for retirement and their Social Security payments are not enough to sustain them. We avoid those conversations until your child texts you, letting you know they've made horrible financial choices and need to return home to get their life together. We confront these conversations when it's too late and the damage is done.

Instead of focusing on the endless list of why we can't, let's change the narrative to consider what might be possible, regardless of how small that course of action might be. Most people struggle with investing because they don't know where to begin. Ideally, investing begins with establishing and sticking to a consistent spending plan and having at least $500 to $1,000 set aside for an unexpected expense or opportunity. We call it a "Get To" fund. Getting a handle on high-interest debt is important, particularly credit card debt, because the interest rates most people pay on their debts tend to be much higher than the average returns they stand to make in the markets.

Mind you, there is a method to the madness. Here's why you need to take these things into consideration. Having a spending plan helps us control our spending and prevent or lessen the impact of a financial shock. Let's say you experience an unexpected financial hardship – roughly 60% of households do – a "Get To" fund will ensure that your spending plan remains unaffected. Unfortunately, when these things aren't in order, you're more likely to pull money away from your investment savings to navigate difficult financial circumstances. Instead of being an investment for your future, it'll quickly become a glorified savings account for the things you need now. One study found that for every dollar that goes into retirement savings, half of it leaves the pot before retirement. I like 50 Cent as a rapper, but I don't want 50 cents or 50 percent leaving my investment. You can't catch a wave, the magic of compound interest, if you are constantly watching all the action from the shore.

Maybe you are ready to get in the game. Consider the following scenarios, with the intent of starting your investment journey and developing confidence:

- I have access to an employer-sponsored retirement plan (401k, 403B, 457, or Thrift Savings Account)
    * Consider what amount you can comfortably invest up to the full employer match – usually between 3 and 5 percent of your gross pay.
    * Evaluate the investment options offered by your job. It's a good idea to learn about index funds that track a Total Market Fund or the S&P 500. All of which should have relatively low fees – .25 basis points or less. Said another way, the fee should be 25 cents or less for every $100 you invest.
    * Ask to speak with a plan sponsor with knowledge of your options.
    * Find an investment choice that appears reasonable to you. Remember, you do not have to be an expert. Tracking the market over time will provide you with consistent and steady returns.
- I have earned income, but I do not have access to an employer-sponsored retirement plan.
    * When you have earned income but no access to an employer-sponsored retirement plan, you then have the option to set up an Individual Retirement Plan (IRA).
    * You'll have the choice between a traditional IRA and a Roth IRA. Both will allow you to invest your after-tax

income into an investment of your choosing. It's a good idea to learn about Total Market or S&P 500 index funds. Both of which provide a considerable amount of diversification.

* With a traditional IRA, you get to write off your contributions for tax purposes for the year in which you make your contributions; however, there are penalties if you decide to withdraw funds from your traditional IRA prior to age 59-and-a-half with a few exceptions. You pay taxes on your earnings in retirement.

* With a Roth IRA, you do not get to write off your contributions for tax purposes. Instead, you pay taxes now, so you do not have to pay taxes later. Another benefit of the Roth IRA is that you can withdraw your contributions – not the money you've made on top of your contributions – without penalty in the event of an emergency. This is never the goal, but life happens.

• No earned income, but I am ready to invest some money.

* Identify how much money you can invest on a weekly basis that does not elicit an emotional response and feels comfortable given the context of your financial circumstances. That can be $1, $5, $25, etc. This is your baseline. The amount doesn't matter right now. You just need to develop the habit and the confidence that comes with the process. You can gradually increase your savings rate from there.

* Google brokerage sites like Vanguard, Fidelity, Schwab, and countless others. Play around with as many as you can find. The goal is to determine which of them is user-friendly and provides information in a way you can follow.

* Take some time to learn about their Total Market and S&P 500 index fund options, all of which should have relatively low fees. As noted above, this is .25 basis points or less, or .25 basis points or 25 cents or less for every $100 you invest.
* Next, go through the process of opening an account with the brokerage firm you like best.
* Then you'll need to fund your brokerage account with the amount you would like to invest at a frequency and amount that is comfortable for you.
* Once your account is funded, you can set it up so you make automated contributions into your investment selection.

- I know I should invest, but I am worried about the markets.
  * First, you are not alone. The markets move up and down in value even though volatility smooths out over time. But now matters, too!
  * You are in luck. As with most things, you have to build your capacity to invest and progressively take on risk as you become comfortable with the markets and establish the financial capacity to take on more market risk.
  * In the meantime, take some to learn about high-yield savings accounts, short-term certificates of deposits, treasury bills, and I Bonds, to name a few.
  * You can Google or ChatGpt any of these options we've discussed. Both search results provide excellent information on each.
  * Once you've found the appropriate savings vehicle, just start the process, extend yourself some grace, and use it as a stepping stone to learn more about the other amazing financial tools at your disposal.

Wow! That was a lot of information, and I don't expect you to digest all of it at once. Take a week or two or three to thoughtfully consider and walk through this outline. Preparing yourself to act is taking action.

Keep in mind, what I've proposed is not investment advice, but rather a framework to help you simplify navigating the investment space. Your situation is unique, and if you feel uncomfortable with making investment decisions on your own, it's OK to ask for help. Again, WE not I.

The Association for Financial Counseling and Planning Education (AFCPE.org) is a great resource. Their professionals can help you with establishing a sound foundation in the areas of money mindset, cash flow management, and debt control. Once you've established a firm foundation, find a fee-only financial planner through organizations like the National Association of Personal Financial Advisors (NAPFA.org). They even have a pro bono (financial planners who volunteer their services) program. There is also the Foundation for Financial Planning (ffpprobono.org) and the Financial Planning Association (financialplanningassociation.org). Let's say that you have the financial resources, but you keep running into mental and emotional roadblocks that prevent you from executing. You are in luck! Financial therapy is a thing. They have a diverse group of extraordinary professionals that stand ready to serve your specific needs (https://financialtherapyassociation.org/).

We should divorce ourselves from the notion of "I" when it comes to wealth creation. Community is the real student. Nobody achieves extraordinary feats alone. Speaking of divorce, it reminds me of this line of thinking from Andre 3000 on "Hollywood Divorce:"

Promise me you gon' stack, promise me you gon' ball
Promise me you'll invest three fourths of it all
For what? So your kids, kids, kids can have some cheese

Now, you may not have the capacity to stack three fourths of it all. I know I don't. Just do your part and encourage others to do the same with kindness and care.

9.
BUYING THE BLOCK

*Conscious investing promotes
mindfulness and learning.*

Teaching is a challenging profession, and it's remarkable how the words a teacher or administrator say to a child may stick with that young person forever.

I was in elementary school and hurried into the building, because I was late. My elementary school principal stopped me.

"Why are you late?" I could barely get a word out.

"I don't want to hear it. You don't care about your education. Your momma doesn't care about your education. She doesn't love you. If she did, she would make sure that you got to school on time."

"Yes, ma'am," I conceded.

I was a target. There were several children who were in a dash that day, but she picked me off, with no compassion or grace.

She didn't ask me if everything was OK. If she had an inkling of concern, she would have learned that I took great pride in punctuality.

Mom worked the graveyard shift at her job, so it was up to me to get my little sister and I ready for school. We were never late – except this morning. I overslept. Thanks to the principal, the whole ordeal made me feel incredibly small and insecure. This well respected leader of our school attacked my family because of her perception of us. As I mentioned earlier, I was perceived as a threat to people outside of my community until proven otherwise. Sadly, I experienced similar treatment in my youth from people who I thought had the capacity to see me.

It took years to get over my principal's harsh words. They cut me so deeply. I already felt like a failure because I struggled so mightily with school. Some days, I just placed my head on my desk, afraid to be recognized. Avoidance was my coping mechanism.

I didn't need that principal to cast aspersions on me, because I had real challenges. I resented her words because the one thing I did right in school was arrive on time, every day, against all odds. Damn, she made me mad!

Prejudice is rooted in arrogance. We've all spoken out of turn in the name of personal bias or misconception. The problem with prejudice is that it creates blind spots in how we view things – people, places, money. We think we're able to see something clearly, and in our arrogance, we turn distorted perception into reality. Most of us don't take the time to thoughtfully analyze what we currently know, even in the presence of new information.

It's possible that this book is causing a shift in your pre-existing beliefs about money, family, or religion. However, this does not necessarily imply that those beliefs are unimportant or invalid. It's likely that they were passed down from someone close to you, but they may also be outdated when it comes to achieving your desired goals. Does what you know align with where you are trying to go?

Wealth creation and new information are kindred spirits. Investing in what you know can become a blind spot when markets and the idea of money itself is rapidly changing. If we only invest in what we know, we deny ourselves the opportunity to unpack and explore things outside of our circles of influence.

Amazon went from a book boutique to a technological juggernaut. What if you only invested in books and not e-commerce? Let's say you grew up in a household of mechanics that didn't think electronic vehicles were possible. You might have scoffed at the idea of Tesla. Maybe you drank Folgers coffee all your life (Could you hear their jingle pop up in the back of your mind? I know I did.), and laughed at the luxurious presentation of Starbucks. Who's laughing now? Our blind spots only allow us to see the world as we know it instead of what the world is starting to become.

I believe that financial vulnerability is the optimal financial growth strategy. This book has extensively covered emotional vulnerability in a way designed to promote healing. That process required us to explore the things we didn't know about ourselves.

We should keep that same energy for investing. "Invest in what you know" is a stagnant financial philosophy. I contend that people should invest in what they have taken the time to understand. Conscious investing promotes mindfulness and learning. It slows the game down and ties the past with the present and future.

Just because you are familiar with something doesn't mean you know it intimately. Some of you have been married for 30 years and don't know your partner. Apologies if I struck a nerve. Let's get back to finances and why I want to talk about buying the block. No, I'm not talking about real estate. If that is your desire, though, my advice is to shadow a mentor who engages in real estate for a year's time while preparing yourself for the opportunity. It would also be wise to consider learning about Real Estate Investment Trusts (REITs) exchange-traded funds using the outline from Chapter 9. Doing this will give you investment exposure to commercial properties that you do not have to manage yourself. The 10-year average annual return for REIT exchange-traded funds is around 10 percent. Remember, you do not have to rush into anything. Go slow to go fast!

When I talk about buying the block, I am talking about the emergence of blockchain technology and cryptocurrency. The most recognizable cryptocurrency is Bitcoin, although there is a vibrant and growing ecosystem in this space. Currently, there are 22,700 projects and counting.

A lot of people are hesitant about considering blockchain technology because of its wild price swings. That trepidation has been justified with a lot of market volatility and speculation. In 2021 alone, Bitcoin seesawed from a high of $62,000 to a low of $30,000, back to a high of $67,000 and back down to $47,000. Its price dropped as low as $15,599 in 2022. That's a crazy roller coaster ride, so I understand and respect someone's position not to invest in crypto. In fact, it's not a suitable investment for anyone who does not already have a well-diversified portfolio and the financial capacity to invest and stay invested for many, many years. When something is in its infancy, there are bound to be growing pains, but does that mean you should completely ignore it? No. Instead, it would be wise to learn more, so you can be open to potential opportunities as regulation becomes clearer and the crypto markets mature.

Most cryptocurrencies that are not Bitcoin are referred to as alternative coins, or altcoins for short. Some of the more well-known altcoins include Ethereum, Polygon, Cardano, and Algorand. However, unlike with traditional investments like publicly traded companies, there is currently very little regulatory oversight in the altcoin space. This lack of oversight means that information about altcoins can be unreliable or even misleading, making it difficult for investors to make informed decisions.

For example, when investing in a publicly traded company, the company is required to undergo an audit by a third party and submit important documentation to the U.S. Securities and Exchange Commission (SEC). This type of oversight is meant to prevent fraudulent activity, which was a major problem during the 1920s and contributed to the Great Depression. In contrast, when evaluating an altcoin investment, investors typically rely on the project's white paper for information. However, this information is usually not audited by a third party, nor is there a requirement for the project to submit documentation to the SEC.

Investing in altcoins requires a deep understanding of blockchain technology, as well as careful due diligence and the ability to regulate one's emotions (taming FOMO). Without these skills, it is easy for unsuspecting investors to fall victim to scams or fraudulent schemes. However, it is important to note that while fraud can occur in the altcoin space, it is not representative of the entire industry.

Let's talk about this space more generally, though. Honestly, what in the world are we dealing with?

A block, on the blockchain, is simply a decentralized store of immutable information, at a given time, that is connected to a long line, or chain of information that uses the most advanced forms of cryptography to provide a secure exchange of data. Nothing more, nothing less. Today, most of your information is already stored on public servers somewhere by some company (a centralized party).

Consider the most precious thing you own right now – your cell phone, of course. We get mad when we lose our phones, not only because they're expensive, but because they contain so much of our personal information. Think of a phone as a rectangular store of information, and depending on the strength of your phone password, it is a secure place for that information.

Here's the primary difference between a block of information on the blockchain and your phone. The block of information on the blockchain is decentralized, which means that these entities known as nodes are confirming and updating the blocks of information stored on the blockchain. Each node has a copy of the chain of information. As a result, nodes serve as the decentralized basis of this technology. Unlike a centralized entity, if one Node fails, you'll still have access to your information so long as one node exists anywhere in the world. Now, they can't see the details of your data. Only you can access that information with what is called a private key.

Imagine a scenario where you are on vacation and lost your phone. But, due to blockchain technology, you were able to buy another phone or log on to an electronic device and instantly restore your data and coverage with a unique code without the need for a service provider. In short, there would be a lot less stress in your life. This is the potential behind the technology. Besides, who even remembers phone numbers these days?

Blockchain technology utilizes data encryption and decryption to secure user information. Encryption makes data unreadable. Decryption converts the data back to readable form. The technology is so secure that it is used by the highest levels of our government to protect sensitive and classified information.

In simpler terms, a block in the blockchain is secure and immutable data that is stored on a network. The blockchain is the connection of secure and transparent transactions stored in a block on a network. For example, I could pay you through a blockchain platform. Once the transaction is done and secured in a block, our transaction is unchangeable, or chained together, in a series of transactions on the blockchain. If I overpaid you, we would simply chain together another event where you would pay me back. That information would be stored transparently and securely in another block of information. The beauty here is that it happens cheaply, securely, and nearly instantaneously.

The technology behind blockchains comes from the integration of engineering, mathematics, and cryptography. Between 2007 and 2009, the Great Recession spurred a worldwide wave of financial calamity. These challenges were exacerbated for Black folks, who were already under financial strain. The national unemployment rate for Black households was nearly 16% during its height, well above the national average.

Satoshi Nakamoto, the author of the paper "Bitcoin: A Peer-to-Peer Electronic Cash System," proposed a **trustless system.** People could engage in financial transactions without depending on the banking system to secure transactions or provide trust so that money can flow freely. When you have a spare moment, please take some time to look up Nakamoto's paper.

So, what is cryptocurrency? Cryptocurrency, like Bitcoin, Ethereum, ADA, and so many others, is a reward that networks pay validators, also called nodes, to confirm transactions on the blockchain.

In a financial transaction, someone in the network, or node, would have to verify the block with your financial transaction and add it to the chain. This leads into concepts such as proof of work, proof of stake, proof of authority, delegate proof of stake, and so on. Basically, different developers are using various forms of technology to operate their networks. Only time will tell which is the best and achieves mass adoption. Many developers are leaning towards proof of stake at the present time, but I don't want to bore you with all those details. Instead, I want you to see a much bigger picture. What started as a trustless, peer-to-peer electronic system has exploded into so much more.

Companies are using blockchain technology to secure the integrity of food. How? By tracking and storing data about the production of food from "farm to table" so people can have confidence in what they're consuming.

Some are using the technology to secure identity, education, and rights of ownership. Let's say someone needed to evacuate their home and left everything behind, physical documents proving their identity, level of education, vaccinations, assets and such. That information can be stored on the blockchain and retrieved instantaneously from anywhere in the world. No phone calls. No runarounds.

Others are using the technology to provide banking services for those without access. In some countries, it is extremely expensive to utilize a bank for basic services, including borrowing. This amounts to a loss of trillions of dollars in economic activity, financial security, and upward mobility. Blockchain technology aims to provide a level playing field to anybody, anywhere.

You've probably heard about smart contracts and NFTs. Smart contracts are digital contracts that execute once certain criteria are met within the contract. Think about the contract as an "If, then" statement. If I execute on this, then I am rewarded with this. Blockchain tech can secure this information. An example of a smart contract might involve health and wellness initiatives at work. Let's say that your employer will pay you a bonus for staying healthy by averaging 5,000 steps every day for an entire year. Blockchain tech can record your step count through wearable technology and execute the payment of your bonus without the assistance of anything or anyone else. The possibilities are virtually endless.

NFTS (non-fungible tokens) are a form of digital content with an underlying smart contract. If you're a creator, you might produce exclusive digital music, art, and film that you release to your audience via an NFT. The owners of the NFT(s) might get special privileges, access, or discounts to content. The creator of the NFT can set it up so that they receive a royalty whenever the NFT is sold. Think about the music industry. Complex accounting must be done to calculate what an artist gets paid. Story after story circulates each year about an artist who was not paid hundreds of thousands of dollars by their record label. NFT transactions on a blockchain are transparent and instantaneously available. As a result, an artist would not only know what they are to be paid, the smart contract will ensure the artist is paid without issue. This is the world of blockchain technology.

I believe blockchain tech and its innovators are architects of the future. If you are afraid to consider this space as an investment, you would never see yourself as a developer or business owner in this space. You would never encourage a child or relative to learn how to code, or send them to a camp that teaches them how to create the technologies and systems of the future. We love *Black Panther* yet fail to appreciate its Afrofuturistic elements.

Even the book you're reading right now is marching into the future, thanks to a company known as Book.io, which aims to empower writers like you and I by granting us ownership of digital assets. The cover page of this book will become an NFT and there will be an underlying smart contract associated with the buying and selling of this book. You are actually participating in the early phases of Blockchain technology, and you didn't even know it.

Take some time to become familiar with the unfamiliar. Your greatest financial victories will likely come from outside what you currently know or what you've always known. **Coinmarketcap.com** is a great resource to start your journey to get to know this space.

Maybe you turned your nose up at me when I mentioned "the block" earlier, just like my elementary school principal did years ago. She failed to see the context of my circumstances or my potential because she was limited by her blind spots. She assumed she knew who I was, but never learned about me.

Her doubts didn't matter, nor did my fears. My mom believed in me and so did my baby sister. I'm Dr. Michael Thomas now, and I'll be studying, buying and building on the block.

10.
BLACK FINANCIAL
CULTURE

*Do you realize you have normalized
a system of trauma?*

A few Octobers ago, my oldest son Triston wanted to be Luke Cage for Halloween. He was nine at the time and had been influenced by the Marvel-based series, which was released in 2016.

Luke Cage might have been the Hero for Hire, but his costumes were not on sale. We had to freelance. We went to the store and picked up a black hoodie, some face paint and a bald cap. I wanted to shave his head to show that he was fully committed to the character. My wife wasn't having it, and neither was my son.

The weekend before Halloween, my son and I detailed his costume. We pierced some holes in his hoodie, which depicted Cage's indestructible skin. We placed the bald cap on his head, then prepared to paint the goatee on his face before he ran to the bathroom.

When he returned with his riddled hoodie, I didn't see my son. I saw Trayvon Martin, and my eyes welled up with tears.

"What's wrong?" my son said.

"Nothing," I responded, and gave him a big bear hug.

I was triggered. My mind raced back to my sister's murder and memories of cleaning out her apartment. There were bullet holes in one of her pillows and through her sheets. The blood stains on the wall near her closet door still showed her silhouette as she sat, grasping for breath, hours before her fiancé returned home and found her clinging for dear life. I replayed that moment in my mind every day until we went to trial.

Where Triston found joy in that costume, I found much-needed clarity. I decided to go to counseling.

It was tough, even for a career counselor. I've sat down with clients and written in this book about the importance of healing. I wasn't ready to unpack my sister's murder, though. I scheduled appointments, then canceled them. I rescheduled and reneged.

Finally, I scheduled a session with a friend of mine who worked as a therapist. I trusted her with my vulnerabilities and no one else. She invited me into her office, made things comfortable, and carefully guided a two-hour-long conversation about the incident.

I told her everything – about the phone call that broke my heart, being saddled with guilt and how lifeless I felt. I remembered a moment when I sat with family and friends around my mom's dinner table only days before the funeral. We laughed and joked, and then the conversation shifted. There were roughly 10 of us at the table and six of us had lost a child, niece, or nephew to senseless violence.

The therapist, who hadn't said anything for a long while, stopped me.

"Michael, do you realize you have normalized a system of trauma?" she said.

"Honestly, I never thought about it that way," I answered. "I had gotten so used to losing people that I tried to compartmentalize and move on. Only in this instance, I can't. I feel stuck."

"You are experiencing some level of post-traumatic stress disorder," my therapist told me. "I want you to know that your mind and body aren't designed to normalize the level of trauma you've experienced. Trauma is not, or shouldn't be, normal or normalized."

That was my breakthrough. Death had numbed me. Cam'Ron had an iconic but calloused line as Rico in *Paid In Full:* "Niggas get shot everyday, B." I would argue that trauma is baked into Black culture, including Black financial culture.

It started with 400 years of chattel slavery, which treated human beings like property. Enslaved people had no individual rights or agency, and could be bought and sold at a moment's notice. This dramatically and traumatically separated family members, including significant others and children from parents.

Entire economic systems were built and thrived as a result of chattel slavery, and enslaved people were used as collateral for business loans, which boosted the fortunes of big business.

Black financial culture harbors an ugly truth. Not only did our labor build financial infrastructure across the world, but our access was inhibited or limited entirely because we were treated like currency, like cattle.

When the Civil War ended, enslaved people received no compensation, but the enslavers who owned land were reimbursed. The reconstruction period designed to make the formerly enslaved whole quickly turned into a period of White violence and supremacy, which yielded the "Black codes" and provided a precursor to Jim Crow.

Black financial culture has a legacy of oppression that includes, but is not limited to, overturning of Special Field Orders No. 15, G.I. Bill exclusion, redlining, unfair hiring practices, voter suppression… I'll stop. All of which, overtime, can have a compounded negative impact on wealth creation. Any sensible and conscientious person, regardless of race or ethnicity, can see how such conditions might yield generations of trauma. I'm reminded of my beautiful mother, who admittedly spent her hard-earned money as a coping mechanism. I know the rigors of racism causes marginalized people to spend as a way to self-medicate.

When we look at our personal history and the history of our country through the lens of trauma, it should inspire a pathway towards empathy. It's unconscionable to think that someone would interrupt a therapy session with this phrasing: "That was so long ago. Can we just move on? Put on your big boy pants and get over it!" Our elders and parents can still recall the traumatic stories of the Civil Rights movement and those that occurred well before.

My great grandmother was born in 1910 and passed away in 2007. I spent a lot of time with her in my youth. During my extended summer stays with her, she would share intimate details about what it meant to be Black in America throughout her lifetime. There were moments when she would burst into tears or had to pivot away from a painful memory while telling a story. I still internalize the injustices she experienced and how she was expected to accept her pain and suffering without uttering a sound. And this is only one person. We aren't considering the collective impact on Black culture – financial culture. What's fascinating is that we lionize certain elements of American history, with good reason, and yet, we sometimes fail to note its brutality, trauma and lasting effects.

So, what is Black financial culture to you? Here are some responses I've collected:

"Black financial culture is consumer-based."
"Black financial culture is established on a make-it-and-spend-it mindset."
"Black financial culture has a hole-in-the-pocket mentality."

"Black financial culture soaks in socioeconomic oppression."
"Black financial culture is focused on the here and now."
"Black financial culture is focused on being flashy."

I read through the responses and thought about the power of stereotypes. What some people perceived to be uniquely Black actually occurred across other races and ethnicities. I have provided financial counseling and coaching services for over a decade. During that time, I have worked with a diverse set of clients – different in race, influence and income. The common thread? Budgeting and money matters were difficult for everyone, not just Black folks. Dave Ramsey built a million-dollar empire that might be tailored as "everyman," but enticed a very specific religious and racial demographic.

I love what I do. I get to take an intimate look at the financial lives of the people I serve. I also get the privilege of understanding the story behind their numbers. In many instances, these stories include some form of trauma, hurt, shame, guilt, or regret. I came to realize that, in many ways, we are more alike than we are different. Black financial culture, as within any culture, falls on a spectrum. It isn't all bad. Nor is it all good. Black financial culture, like Black people, isn't monolithic. It is as colorful and vibrant as Black culture itself.

The responses also made me contemplate the differences between being broke and suffering from brokenness. It's easy to fix someone being broke, but addressing the brokenness a person feels requires a completely different process and frame of mind. When someone is making financial decisions because they lack a certain skill set or natural habit, that's one thing. Financial choices being made out of brokenness, pain, or hopelessness are altogether different.

The nature of the Black experience demands that we start looking beyond the numbers and addressing the heart of our issues, wisely discerning what we can and cannot control. Otherwise, feelings of brokenness may fester and diminish the opportunity for wealth creation at a rate much greater than inflation ever will. Most of us desire wealth to fuel our dreams and to save our families.

Tiara was full of dreams. She was poised to graduate from college and had just gotten engaged to a good brotha, Marqtell Robinson. When I heard the tragedy of Breonna Taylor, how she was engaged and aspired to be a nurse, I thought about my sister.

Tiara's death broke our entire family. The only way for me to deal with my brokenness was through forgiveness. I forgave Kevin because the alternative was to be consumed by sorrow and rage. My brokenness affected my responsibilities as a husband and father.

Forgiving Kevin does not absolve him. He was sentenced to life in prison for the murder of my sister. Had I refused to heal my brokenness, I would have served a life of darkness.

How do we move from surviving to thriving as a community of people? History is our guide. We should appreciate the sacrifices of our elders, their sense of necessity and ingenuity. "I may not get there with you," Martin Luther King said in his famous and final speech. "But I want you to know tonight, that we, as a people, will get to the Promised Land."

We must tap into our ancestors' sense of necessity and ingenuity, with the hopes of making life better for our children, our children's children, and so forth. Black financial culture has the freedom to evolve and chart a new path forward. More importantly, Black financial culture has the capacity to create the conditions and opportunities that lead to sustainable wealth creation.

I believe that you and your family, despite where you've come from, are vital to the collective success of the Black financial culture. With that being said, we must forgive the past while not forgetting our history. We can forgive our nation and still seek reparations. We can forgive those who've hurt us and set boundaries. We can forgive ourselves for not living up to our promise, knowing that we are continually being refined, not defined, by our past.

Sure, forgiveness is a financial strategy. And yet, my reasons for writing this book are less about money, and more about you. Money is not the main thing. You are.

WE are.

11.
WHERE DO WE GO
FROM HERE?

*The Where is as equally
important as the Why.*

The final book that Dr. King wrote shared the same title as this final chapter, except he left us with a choice – chaos or community? I choose community. I love my people.

The sankofa bird reminds me of my deep and abiding love for us, along with our vital need for wisdom. The sankofa is the Ghanaian symbol for a mythical bird that has two feet facing forward, while its head twists back to grab an egg and bring it into the present. San means "to return," Ko means "the past," Fa means "to look or seek."

The wisdom of the Ghanaians, specifically, the Akan people, encourages us to look to the past as a way to provide guidance and wisdom for our future. The Akans believe there must be movement and new learning as time passes. Will you join me in an incredibly powerful activity?

I want you to grab a pencil and paper. Draw a circular tabletop, then write down all the messages you remember about money growing up.

Mom always said, "You might as well get what you want. You can't take it with you." Another classic: "It's my money. I do what I want with it." These phrases may seem harmless, but repetitive messages like these are sticky and influence our own beliefs and attitudes about money.

Maybe no sayings come to mind. Think of your earliest experiences with money, whether directly or indirectly, and what it means to you.

One summer, we had plans to go to Six Flags Great America in Chicago. Those plans were allegedly halted because a family member stole the money set aside for vacation. I was broken and internalized this message – "never trust family with money."

Write your experiences with money on the circular tabletop, whether positive or negative. Now, select the top three or four messages that have influenced you the most. Add three or four legs to your tabletop that represent those messages. Beneath each leg, write down the name of a person or experience responsible for those messages. Underneath each name or experience, I want you to write the question, "Why?"

I want you to unpack that message or experience. Why did this person share this commentary with you? Why did you internalize this message or experience so profoundly?

Here's another question to write down. "Where?"

This inquiry represents the sticky substance that binds us to the messages we tell ourselves about money. The "where" gets us to the heart of the matter. It encourages us to engage in deep and thoughtful consideration without guilt, shame, or judgment about the circumstances of the past. Empathy, compassion, and connection are able to flourish in the "where."

Ever had someone blow up on you without a good reason? We tend to ask, "Where did that come from?" We already instinctively know that something much deeper is going on beneath the surface to cause a person to act out of character in such a way. Knowing that it must be something else helps us keep calm and collected.

When we ask healthy questions, the hope is to yield healthy connections. Reach out to at least one of the people who you consider a strong influence on your financial philosophy. Tell them about this book and your findings. Allow them to share their story and the emotion behind their words.

Healthy questions beget healthy connections, which sets the stage for healthy context. It is likely that the financial messages of the past have roots in something meaningful to that person or event. It's hard to understand the full context of something as a child. Time might not heal all wounds, but it should reveal perspectives that help us grow as a community of people.

I used this process to explore a person's money scripts with a client a few years ago. She always remembered that her great-grandfather, with whom she had spent a lot of time, had the tendency to hoard things. He encouraged her to be thrifty and to never waste anything because you never knew when you were going to need it.

She experienced anxiety as an adult whenever she threw things away. She felt like she was being wasteful. When she reached out to her grandmother, she learned that her great-grandfather hoarded things because he and his family were devastated by the Great Depression. That experience completely changed the dynamic of their family tree. Her grandmother hoarded. Her mother hoarded. And now she hoarded.

The lifestyle of stockpiling was essential for my client's great-granddad, but not for her current standard of living.

This dynamic brings me back to Black financial culture. There were so many courageous things that Black households did to survive and that necessity was passed down from generation to generation. Yet the question remains: *Where do we go from here?*

Let's revisit our circular tabletop. Draw three or four lines up from the financial messages you wrote on top. At the tip of each of these lines, please write, "Black financial culture" and number them.

Reflect on the generational stories and how those people or experiences affect the way you manage money today. Think carefully about what impact you want to have on the financial culture in your family and the messages you want to pass along to the next generation. What needs to stay? What needs to go? What should you add?

Now, as descriptively as you would like, write down what you desire the Black financial culture to be in your family for future generations. Regardless of what you decide, it's your choice. Black financial culture, if nothing else, is your right to express economic agency. The agency – freedom of conscience – is the thing.

Are you clear on your vision? Great. Still, the question remains for many of us: *Where do we go from here?*

Good news! There is no guilt or shame in not knowing. Why? Not knowing forces us to tap into being vulnerable, which should encourage us to learn more and ask for help.

There is so much that I did not include in this book because I did not want to overwhelm you with charts, calculations or figures. Oh, but I DO want to share those things with you! I'll be creating a *Black Financial Culture* page on YouTube to utilize interactive and visual aids. You will be able to find helpful information on credit management, estimating the value of a college education, navigating financial aid, understanding the basics of investing and so much more. If you are looking for an excellent resource that will help you start the process of reimagining Black financial culture for generations to come, we welcome the opportunity to be of service to you and your entire family.

We have more power than we think. Let's own it – together!

12.
FINISH WHAT YOU START: AN EPILOGUE

*It's not how you start,
it's how you finish.*

A recent study found that less than half of adult readers ever finish a book they start, and yet, here we are. Thank you for reading.

I used to be the type of person who couldn't say "no." I committed myself to countless tasks because I didn't want to disappoint people. Those same people were ultimately disappointed because I failed to follow through on my promises. I wanted to complete these missions, but I lacked the courage to compartmentalize.

The same thing can happen after reading a book on personal finance – like this one. The excitement about what this information can mean for your friends and family becomes overwhelming. You become the chief financial literacy expert for your inner circles, but the people around you aren't ready for the message. I call this the "saved effect":

Have you ever experienced a fresh, straight-out-of-the-baptismal pool, saved, sanctified, and filled-with-the-holy-ghost Christian?

They didn't want to talk about anything but Jesus. They wanted to tell you how you are not living right or how much you need Jesus.

They may have even told you that heaven and hell are real and that they don't want you to go to hell. Meanwhile, you are thinking in the back of your mind, "Wasn't I the one trying to get you to go to church for the past 10 years?"

If you were this person or experienced this person, you realized, at some point, how annoying that person can be. Instead of ushering you to the life-giving power of the cross, they were pushing you closer and closer to hell's flames.

We do the same thing with personal finances!

Some of us were once in debt up to our eyeballs, living paycheck to paycheck and constantly robbing Peter to pay Paul. Then, suddenly, you had a change of heart. You decided to get your finances in order. You cleaned up your credit and started investing. Now that you've been anointed with the divine healing power of the budget, you feel called to share the good news.

Now you tell people how they don't need that latte or that credit cards are the devil. In fact, you've become so passionate about your beliefs that you no longer see people. You only see the waywardness of their awful spending habits.

They need to be saved like you, right?

You might be well-intentioned in your efforts, but remember that you were once in a place where you did not want to hear all the useful financial advice that had been offered to you over the years. You wanted to live your life, on your own terms, without interference.

Why didn't you listen? Why couldn't you hear? Why did you resist change?

It could be several things, but someone trying to pester you into submission more than likely did not change your heart. As with listening to an overly zealous person about their faith, you probably felt further — not closer — to God after the conversation ended.

So, yes, you might be right that some people need to improve their financial behaviors; however, people don't change because of *what we say. They change because of what they see us do. As in, they see us consistently and joyfully living the life they hope for. They see our peace, calm, patience, experiences, and generosity. They see us as the type of person who can be confided in without judgment and pretense. They see us as a symbol of hope and the evidence of faith.*

One of my favorite quotes comes from Saint Francis of Assisi, "Preach the gospel everywhere. When necessary, use words."

Instead of preaching to people and using every opportunity to tell them what they are doing wrong with their money, try speaking to their soul by walking in your financial convictions.

If we are going to have a real impact on Black financial culture, we must start with ourselves. Everyone might not share the sense of conviction and urgency you have after reading this book. My only ask is that you do not place undue financial burden on someone else. Respect and maintain boundaries, but prioritize connection, grace and patience in your relationships. Malcolm X put it this way: "We need more light about each other. Light creates understanding, understanding creates love, love creates patience, and patience creates unity." I know that a good example – living in action – will outweigh any commentary.

I love my mom. I always wanted to be her blessing, never her burden. That's why I never ridiculed or picked at any financial choice she made. Honestly, I rarely offered her financial insight unless she asked. Plus she's been through so damn much. She lost her mother at an early age and her father deteriorated into drunkenness. She was told that she would never amount to anything.

"Don't" and "can't" were ingrained in my mom, and she communicated that trauma to me and Tiara. One particular evening, my sister and I fought over TV programming. She wanted to watch cartoons, while I wanted to watch *The Cosby Show.* We fought so furiously that my mom intervened, and she chose cartoons.

I didn't think that was fair. I did something out of character – I pressed her on the issue. Mom was annoyed. "Your sister is getting the TV, and Black people don't live like that, anyway!" My immediate thought was, "Live like what?"

I watched *The Cosby Show* because Dr. Clair Huxtable was *fine*. Phylicia Rashad was my celebrity crush, and Mom was being a hater. I didn't understand the depths of her content until I became older.

"Don't" and "can't" are byproducts of trauma. They are constricting contractions that choke out hope. When I played sports, some of my Black coaches said we couldn't beat those "white boys." I played video games, and was so good that I won the *Donkey Kong Country* contest at my local Blockbuster (Google it – LOL!). The prize? Free rentals for a year! So many people tried to talk me out of that competition. I remember when I first got into investing during my high school years. There were people from my community who told me that the things I was talking about were White people stuff. The constant fear mongering was suffocating.

Black people can't do this, Black people don't do that. A Black man as President? Don't even try it.

My wife and I attended a watch party during President Barack Obama's first presidential run. I walked through the door and past some oldheads. They judged me off the bat and treated me like I wasn't "Black enough."

Look. I'm from Gary, Indiana. My outward presentation might not say "hood," but that's to assume that someone who looks, talks and acts like me can't come from it.

I couldn't even chop it up with the old heads before one of them blurted out, "Who did you vote for?" Vibe check. Black card check.

"Who else would I vote for?" I quickly replied.

I sat with those gentlemen for hours. We drank plenty of brown liquor, played spades and even had the nerve to break out the bones. Black-ass watch party. One of the oldheads tried me again.

"Oh, you know how to play this, too?" I just smirked.

Things got a bit more serious as the polling numbers rolled in, and "don't" and "can't" walked their hating asses through the door.

"I hope he doesn't become the President," someone said. "I like Barack Obama. But I am afraid that someone is going to kill him." Mom had a similar message for me as a child: "Bullets don't have eyes."

Trauma is loud. Fear becomes fact, and with good reason for Black folks. We've been through so much as a people. And then Barack won.

The mood of that party went from uncomfortably fearful to cautiously joyful. There were shouts of pure happiness, praises unto the most-high God, and an overflow of tears. Even the gentleman who mentioned that he didn't want Barack Obama to become the President of the United States became misty-eyed. It was one of the most authentic moments I've experienced with a group of strangers. It was *real.*

My point is this. Someone has to take the first step. Barack Obama. Martin Luther King Jr. Harriet Tubman. You. Overcoming adversity is our culture – our legacy.

As you move forward in your financial journey, promise me that you will be compassionate with yourself and anyone else you might want to bring along for the ride. If you aren't ready to move just yet, that's okay. If someone you know isn't ready, it's okay. We all have internal devices that we have to unpack, wrestle with, and repurpose before we are able to take courage and pursue our financial goals with confidence and conviction.

Sometimes, we must go slow before we are able to go fast. And that's okay too. That's why I've spent so much time speaking about wealth creation as a process that works from the inside out, and not the other way around.

We are at the nexus of all possibilities, a place where we can experience the fullness of Black financial culture, and Blackness overall. We just need to put down judgment, shame and guilt, and pick up empathy, grace and compassion.

Someone has to take the first step. "Faith is taking the first step, even when you don't see the whole staircase," Dr. King said. Are you ready to be the example for yourself and your family on what it means to go all in? Will you be the catalyst who transforms Black financial culture for you and yours?

Yes, you can.

ACKNOWLEDGEMENTS

I wish to express my gratitude to those who made this book possible. First and foremost, I thank God for planting the idea in my heart. My deepest desire is that this book touches the hearts and minds of those for whom it was intended.

I am indebted to my wife Ashlee for her unwavering support, and to my two boys Triston and Sebastian for their constant encouragement.

Writing is a challenging endeavor, and I am grateful to Jerra Mitchell for helping me get the ball rolling, Ken Makin and Erik Schmidt for their editing assistance.

I also want to acknowledge the people who pushed me to persevere when I faced obstacles: Dr. Kenneth White, Jerome Singleton, Dr. Justin Adeyemi, Alan Gaines, and Jason Johnson.

I want to thank my mother Lisa Smith-Rodriguez for everything she has done for me. I owe my existence to her, and I love her deeply. To KJ, Jayden, and Brooklyn, I hope this book provides you with guidance and hope when you decide to revisit the loss of your mother. You are her legacy. Live it!